Sermons by Jonathan Edwards on the Epistle to the Galatians

Sermons by Jonathan Edwards on the Epistle to the Galatians

EDITED BY
Kenneth P. Minkema,
Adriaan C. Neele,
and Allen M. Stanton

WITH AN INTRODUCTION BY
Wilson H. Kimnach

 CASCADE *Books* • Eugene, Oregon

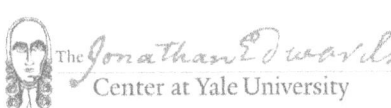

SERMONS BY JONATHAN EDWARDS ON THE EPISTLE TO
THE GALATIANS

Copyright © 2019 Kenneth P. Minkema, Adriaan C. Neele, and Allen M. Stanton. All rights reserved. Except for brief quotations in critical publications or reviews, no part of this book may be reproduced in any manner without prior written permission from the publisher. Write: Permissions, Wipf and Stock Publishers, 199 W. 8th Ave., Suite 3, Eugene, OR 97401.

Cascade Books
An Imprint of Wipf and Stock Publishers
199 W. 8th Ave., Suite 3
Eugene, OR 97401

www.wipfandstock.com

PAPERBACK ISBN: 978-1-5326-8597-2
HARDCOVER ISBN: 978-1-5326-8598-9
EBOOK ISBN: 978-1-5326-8599-6

Cataloguing-in-Publication data:

Names: Edwards, Jonathan, 1703–1758, author | Kimnach, Wilson, introduction writer | Minkema, Kenneth P., editor | Neele, Adriaan C., editor | Stanton, Allen M., editor

Title: Sermons by Jonathan Edwards on the epistle to the Galatians / edited by Kenneth P. Minkema, Adriaan C. Neele, Allen M. Stanton, with an introduction by Wilson H. Kimnach.

Description: Eugene, OR: Pickwick Publications, 2019 | Series: The Sermons of Jonathan Edwards | Includes bibliographical references and index.

Identifiers: ISBN 978-1-5326-8597-2 (paperback) | ISBN 978-1-5326-8598-9 (hardcover) | ISBN 978-1-5326-8599-6 (ebook)

Subjects: LCSH: Bible—Galatians—Sermons | Sermons of Jonathan Edwards/Jonathan Edwards | Jonathan Edwards, 1703–1758 | Preaching—United States—History—18th century

Classification: BX7233.E42 E39 2019 (paperback) | BX7233.E42 (ebook)

Manufactured in the U.S.A.   08/13/19

CONTENTS

List of Contributors / vii

Preface / ix

    Introduction: Edwards the Preacher / 1

    Introduction: Historical Context / 15

    Only that Sort of Faith that Works by Love Avails Anything before God (Gal. 5:6, 1728) / 22

    Christ's Particular Respect to Every Believer in His Work of Redemption (Gal. 2:20, 1728–29) / 39

    The Gospel No Encouragement to Sin (Gal. 2:17, 1731–32) /| 57

    Flesh and Spirit (Gal. 5:17, 1745) / 90

    Christ and Believers One Mystical Person (Gal. 3:16, 1746) / 108

    The Holy Spirit the Sum of the Blessings Purchased for Us by Christ (Gal. 3:13, 1746) / 120

    Saving Faith Worketh by Love (Gal. 5:6, 1751) / 133

LIST OF CONTRIBUTORS

Dr. Wilson H. Kimnach is the Presidential Professor in the Humanities (Emeritus), Bridgeport University, and General Sermon Editor of *The Works of Jonathan Edwards*.

Dr. Kenneth P. Minkema is the Executive Editor and Director of the Jonathan Edwards Center, Yale University, and a member of the Research Faculty at Yale Divinity School.

Dr. Adriaan C. Neele is Director of the Doctoral Program and Professor of Historical Theology at Puritan Reformed Theological Seminary, and Consulting Digital Editor at the Jonathan Edwards Center at Yale University.

Allen M. Stanton is a PhD Candidate (Historical Theology) at Puritan Reformed Theological Seminary, and pastor of Pinehaven Presbyterian Church, Clinton, Mississippi.

PREFACE

THIS VOLUME OF *SERMONS BY JONATHAN EDWARDS ON THE EPISTLE TO the Galatians* contains previously unpublished sermons by Edwards on the Epistle to the Galatians, generally attributed to the apostle Paul. Edwards preached these sermons during his Northampton pastorate, and re-preached some of them, between 1728 and 1751. The importance of the Epistle to the Galatians has been recognized throughout the Christian practice of preaching. As such, these sermons have significance for its place in the Protestant tradition since the Reformation, but they also highlight Edwards' thought on the nature of faith and works, flesh and spirit, Christ and the Holy Spirit. To assist the reader, preceding the sermons are two introductions that describe Edwards' preaching style and method, and provide an historical context for the sermons themselves.

A NOTE OF EDWARDS' TEXT

Edwards' sermons *on the Epistle to the Galatians* is printed here in full for the first time from the original manuscripts as transcribed and edited by the staff of the Jonathan Edwards Center at Yale University. In presenting these texts, the editors have followed the conventions of the Yale Edition of The Works of Jonathan Edwards (twenty-six volumes, 1957–2008), regularizing spelling, capitalization, and format. Preserved here are Edwards' own words, punctuated in an eighteenth-century style. Because the manuscript was largely uncorrected by Edwards—it was, after all, for his personal use for public delivery—there are inconsistencies in number, style, and tense, which, as a rule, are left as they are; any changes are footnoted. In any given manuscript there are a great number of deletions, so here only deletions of significant textual importance are footnoted.

Preface

    Readers may find Edwards' manner of writing challenging at first, but we believe the effort to understand Edwards in his own terms, in his own idiom, and to get a sense of the immediacy of his preaching, will be rewarded. Finally, Scripture quotes are rendered according to the King James Bible, which was the version Edwards used. One feature of the text presented below bears special explanation: cases of editorial interpolation. These are of two types. First, outright omissions by Edwards, and lacunae in the manuscript, are filled by insertions in square brackets ([,]). Secondly, one aspect of the outlinish nature of some of the sermons is easily seen in the many dashes of varying lengths that Edwards drew at the beginning, in the middle, and at the end of statements. These dashes represent repeated words or phrases, as well as connective pieces of sentences that Edwards would have provided extemporaneously. Where these dashes have been editorially amplified, they are surrounded by curly brackets ({,}).

    The manuscripts are in the Edwards Collection, Beinecke Rare Book and Manuscript Library, Yale University. Transcripts may be viewed on the Jonathan Edwards Center's website, edwards.yale.edu. The Introduction by Wilson H. Kimnach is adapted from his larger discussion of "Jonathan Edwards' Art of Prophesying" in The Works of Jonathan Edwards, 10, Sermons and Discourses, 1720–1723 (New Haven: Yale University Press, 1990), 21–27, 36–42.

INTRODUCTION
Edwards the Preacher

Wilson H. Kimnach

EDWARDS' THOUGHTS ON PREACHING

JONATHAN EDWARDS WAS IN FULL AGREEMENT WITH HIS TEACHERS respecting the exalted status of the preacher. For though his writings occasionally contain references to "earthen vessels" and sometimes emphasize the preacher's humble situation as a son of Adam, it is much more common for Edwards to see the preacher as a man exalted and even transfigured by his calling. Indeed, in some of the earliest entries in his "Miscellanies," nos. mm, qq, and 40, Edwards attempts to define to his own satisfaction the nature of the call, the limits and quality of a minister's influence in society, and the power in preaching or teaching the divine Word.

> Yet it is clear that those that are in the New Testament called ministers are not every private Christian, and consequently if [any] such remain now as are there spoken of, they are distinct from other Christians. 'Tis clear they are born undistinguished; from this 'tis clear they are distinguished afterwards. 'Tis also evident that they are distinguished some way or other by Christ ...[1]

---

1. "Miscellanies" no. *mm*, in *Works of Jonathan Edwards*, 13, *"Miscellanies," a-500*, ed. Thomas A. Schafer (New Haven: Yale University Press, 1994), 187. After initial citation, volumes in *The Works of Jonathan Edwards* (New Haven: Yale University Press, 1957–2008) will be referred to as *"WJE"* plus volume and page numbers. Texts by JE published in the Jonathan Edwards Center's website (edwards.yale.edu) will be referred

This earliest entry on the office of the preacher calls attention to the essentially aristocratic bias of Edwards, which is quite in keeping with his upbringing, while it also demonstrates his characteristic propensity to rethink every important aspect of his life "from the ground up," regardless of his background and training. He may not seriously question the assumptions of his heritage, but he will insist upon a personal formulation of that heritage in his own written words.

The preacher is, then, a "chosen one" with a distinct charisma as a result of his call to serve Christ. He is invested with a capacity and right to instruct, lead, and judge his people;[2] he has no pretension to civil authority, but in the all-important moral and spiritual realms he is, of all human beings, supremely authoritative. "Miscellanies" no. 40 contains early speculations upon the powers that would inhere in the effective preaching of the Word, specifically:

> Without doubt, ministers are to teach men what Christ would have them to do, and to teach them who doth these things and who doth them not; that is, who are Christians and who are not ...
>
> Thus, if I in a right manner am become the teacher of a people, so far as they ought to hear what I teach them, so much power I have. Thus, if they are obliged to hear me only because they themselves have chosen me to guide them, and therein declared that they thought me sufficiently instructed in the mind of Christ to teach them, and because I have the other requisites of being their teacher, then I have power as other ministers have in these days. But if it was plain to them that I was under the infallible guidance of Christ, then I should have more power. And if it was plain to all the world of Christians that I was under the infallible guidance of Christ, and [that] I was sent forth to teach the world the will of Christ, then I should have power in all the world. I should have power to teach them what they ought to do, and they would be obliged to hear me; I should have power to teach them who were Christians and who not, and in this likewise they would be obliged to hear me.[3]

As in a daydream, the student-preacher toys with the mystery of the call, and at least by implication ponders the limits and possibilities of the role of a preacher. Could he command the people, or even the world,

---

to as "*WJEO*" plus the volume number.

2. *WJE* 13:188 (qq. Ministers).
3. *WJE* 13:222 (40.Ministers).

as a divine messenger? Obviously, there must be some immediate sign, some quality of utterance, that would in itself attest to the supernatural ordination. In this early passage Edwards is already pondering aspects of sermonic style, but characteristically he begins on the most general and profound, most philosophical level. Puritan ministers had always been urged to "preach powerfully," but in this meditation there are new undertones, and "power" clearly relates to a divine investiture that transcends conventional sectarian sanctions. Certainly it seems that Edwards was as well fitted to study the art of preaching under the imperious Solomon Stoddard, his grandfather and predecessor as the pastor of Northampton, Massachusetts, as any man.

Edwards did not pretend to eloquence or a fine style. Indeed, from the first he seems to have made a point of proclaiming his lack of a fine style.

> [T]he practical discourses that follow ... now appear in that very plain and unpolished dress in which they were first prepared and delivered; which was mostly at a time when the circumstances of the auditory they were preached to, were enough to make a minister neglect, forget, and despise such ornaments as politeness and modishness of style and method, when coming as a messenger from God to souls deeply impressed with a sense of their danger of God's everlasting wrath, to treat with them about their eternal salvation. However unable I am to preach or write politely, if I would, yet I have this to comfort me under such a defect; that God has showed us that he don't need such talents in men to carry on his own work, and that he has been pleased to smile upon and bless a very plain, unfashionable way of preaching. And have we not reason to think that it ever has been, and ever will be, God's manner to bless the foolishness of preaching to save them that believe, let the elegance of language, and excellency of style, be carried to never so great a height, by the learning and wit of the present and future ages?

This passage, from the Preface to *Discourses on Various Important Subjects* (1738),[4] is characteristic of the tone of most of Edwards' prefaces, though the discussion is a little more explicit and fully developed. It is defensive, condemning wit and style out of hand as irrelevant to effective preaching, while also suggesting an incapacity for stylistic excellence on his own part.

---

4. *WJE* 19:797.

Part of this may be explained by Edwards' cultural background that would have taught him to think of rhetoric or eloquence as a thing separable from the logical structure of an argument.[5] Since he was consciously developing a heart-piercing manner of writing that would be as spare and efficient as an arrow, he assumed that "style," being an adventitious decoration, would have to be left out. It would not have struck Edwards that that efficacious verbal expression for which he constantly strove and "style" might be the same thing. Thus he really could spend much of his lifetime studying the theory and practice of language and metaphor without "paying any attention to style." Of course, part of the problem is also that, as in the seventeenth century, preaching styles were associated with theological positions. In Edwards' day many of the most eloquent preachers of the East were suspect in Edwards' eyes of being rationalist, Arminian, or just theologically jejune. He would therefore rather deny excellence in his carefully wrought sermons than be thought—perhaps even by himself—to be a creature of wit and style. He was too serious, too full of thought, and too honest for *style*.

Indeed, if Edwards claimed brilliance of any kind it was the more essential and "substantial" excellence of thought, and once again he saw himself as being out of tune with the times:

> Our discovering the absurdity of the impertinent and abstruse distinctions of the School Divines, may justly give us a distaste

---

5. The peculiar attitude that assumes substance and expression to be distinct and separable was quite widespread in the seventeenth century and occasioned the birth of the "plain style" among preachers and "mathematical plainness" in the Royal Society. While a detailed survey of this significant aspect of JE's cultural background is beyond the scope of this introduction, it should be stated that the crucial factor in that background seems to have been the philosophy of Peter Ramus. With the aid of his colleague, Omer Talon, Ramus devised a new formulation of the relationship between logic and rhetoric, involving the transfer of the classical (Ciceronian) invention, disposition, and memory from the province of rhetoric to that of dialectic. This left only style, apprehended as a matter of figures and tropes, and delivery to rhetoric; rhetoric became the sideshow to thought, a crowd-pleasing (or even crowd-deluding) device. Thus, those who were intent upon the intellectual substance of their expression or were intensely earnest, such as Puritan preachers and the new scientists, tended to condemn and avoid "style" as something adventitious and frivolous. Moreover, those who cultivated rhetoric during the seventeenth century actually did tend to artificiality and ornateness, as might be expected when figures and tropes are seen more or less as ends in themselves. For a detailed discussion of the history behind JE's attitude, and an investigation of the long groping toward what we should today call an organic style, see Wilbur S. Howell's *Logic and Rhetoric in England, 1500–1700* (Princeton: Princeton University Press, 1956).

of such distinctions as have a show of learning in obscure words, but convey no light to the mind; but I can see no reason why we should also discard those that are clear and rational, and can be made out to have their foundation in truth.

In the same Preface,[6] in a sustained argument of two pages, he defends the virtue of "real" fine distinctions in elaborating the "mysteries" of religion. If, as Cotton Mather contended in *Manuductio ad Ministerium* (1726), his instruction manual for aspiring ministers, that reason is natural to the soul of man, then Edwards would have him test this capacity, as he would fully exercise the heart, in the quest of a valid apprehension of divine truths.

Edwards may have been inspired by the example of his father Timothy Edwards, minister of East Windsor, Connecticut, to use the utmost rigor in making convicting arguments, and Stoddard undoubtedly provided the pattern for a potent, "psychological" rhetoric for which Edwards had no name. But having a finer mind and more imagination than either Stoddard or Timothy Edwards, Edwards outperformed each at his specialty while combining elements of both their strategies. His intense interest in the mysterious power of language, however, was apparently innate.

Edwards' matured vision of the ideal preacher is most completely delineated in his ordination sermon on John 5:35, entitled *The True Excellency of a Minister of the Gospel* (1744).[7] There, he insists that a minister must be "both a burning and a shining light"; that "his heart burn with love to Christ, and fervent desires of the advancement of his kingdom and glory," and that "his instructions [be] clear and plain, accommodated to the capacity of his hearers, and tending to convey light to their understandings." This peculiar combination of head and heart, he insists, is absolutely necessary to the success of a preacher:

> When light and heat are thus united in a minister of the gospel, it shows that each is genuine, and of a right kind, and that both are divine. Divine light is attended with heat; and so, on the other hand, a truly divine and holy heat and ardor is ever accompanied with light.

That both heat and light may be acquired by the aspiring preacher, Edwards urges him to be "diligent in [his] studies," "very conversant with

6. *WJE* 19:795–96.
7. *WJE* 25:82–102.

the holy Scriptures," and "much in seeking God, and conversing with him by prayer, who is the fountain of light and love." All in all, Edwards' ideal does not seem to be very different from that of the traditional preacher of the time, except that in the full context of the sermon and through the extensive use of light imagery, he suggests a standard of transcendent dedication and nearly mystical fervor that is rare in any age. And like Stoddard before him, Edwards cultivated a subtle personal tone in his rhetoric that, more than any stated principle, demonstrates the risk-taking commitment demanded of the good preacher.

Edwards is best known for his defenses of passionate emotion, including "hellfire," in revival preaching. And, indeed, in *Religious Affections* he argues that "such means are to be desired, as have much of a tendency to move the affections."[8] Moreover, in *Some Thoughts on the Revival of Religion in New England*, he emphatically insists that

> Though . . . clearness of distinction and illustration, and strength of reason, and a good method, in the doctrinal handling of the truths of religion, is many ways needful and profitable, and not to be neglected. . . . Our people don't so much need to have their heads stored, as to have their hearts touched; and they stand in the greatest need of that sort of preaching that has the greatest tendency to do this.[9]

As for "hellfire" preaching in particular, Edwards argues:

> Some talk of it as an unreasonable thing to think to fright persons to heaven; but I think it is a reasonable thing to endeavor to fright persons away from hell . . . 'tis a reasonable thing to fright a person out of an house on fire.

As for the style or manner of "hellfire" preaching, he makes this observation:

> When ministers preach of hell, and warn sinners to avoid it, in a cold manner, though they may say in words that it is infinitely terrible; yet (if we look on language as a communication of our minds to others) they contradict themselves; for actions, as I observed before, have a language to convey our minds, as well as words; and at the same time that such a preacher's words represents the sinner's state as infinitely dreadful, his behavior and manner of

---

8. *WJE* 2:121.
9. *WJE* 4:387–88.

speaking contradict it, and show that the preacher don't think so; so that he defeats his own purpose; for the language of his actions, in such a case, is much more effectual than the bare signification of his words.[10]

Edwards might well have extended this comment to include the "gesture of language"—specifically, images and metaphors employed in making an argument concrete—in the case of printed sermons.

In summary, it should be observed that, while Edwards placed no limits on the intensity of emotion that a preacher might attempt to evoke through his preaching, he insisted upon a constant balance and aesthetically pleasing harmony between emotion and thought. Indeed, he insisted that without a duly precise and comprehensive body of theological concepts in the sermon, there is no religion at all.[11]

Edwards' ideal preacher is, then, a figure of commanding intellectual rigor and overwhelming rhetorical power; he strikes a blow for religion simultaneously in the heads and hearts of his auditors, though with an emphasis upon the heart. In the performance of his duty, he shows that he is the peculiarly designated servant of his Master:

> They should imitate [Christ] in the manner of his preaching; who taught not as the Scribes, but with authority, boldly, zealously and fervently; insisting chiefly on the most important things in religion, being much in warning men of the danger of damnation, setting forth the greatness of the future misery of the ungodly; insisting not only on the outward, but also the inward and spiritual duties of religion: being much in declaring the great provocation and danger of spiritual pride, and a self-righteous disposition; yet much insisting on the necessity and importance of inherent holiness, and the practice of piety. . . . wonderfully adapting his discourse to persons, seasons and occasions.[12]

If a congregation could "hear and stand it out" under such preaching, there would probably be little hope for the English language as an instrument of salvation.

---

10. *WJE* 4:247–48.

11. For an extended discussion of JE's ideas on the necessity of intellectual substance in sermons, see his sermon, *The Importance and Advantage of a Thorough Knowledge of Divine Truth*, in *WJE* 22:80–102.

12. *Christ the Example of Ministers*, *WJE* 25:339.

Sermons by Jonathan Edwards on the Epistle to the Galatians

THE SERMON IN EDWARDS' HANDS

The development and ultimate deterioration of the sermon form in Edwards' hands will be discussed shortly, but now an attempt must be made to define the formal limits of the Edwardsean sermon at the zenith of its development during the late 1720s, the 1730s, and the very early 1740s (and whenever Edwards had an important preaching occasion in subsequent years and returned to that form and style).[13] This sermon is a formal literary unit consisting of three main divisions, Text, Doctrine, and Application. There is only one significant variation in the form which is called a "lecture." The lecture is differentiated from the sermon only through the altered proportions in the Doctrine and Application. For whereas in the sermon the Application is usually a little longer than the Doctrine and often several times as long, in the lecture the Doctrine is substantially longer than the Application. Perhaps the best-known instance of the lecture variant is *A Divine and Supernatural Light* (1734), which has a doctrine of twenty-three pages, and an Application of a little over three pages in the first edition.

Otherwise, so far as *form* is concerned, a sermon is a sermon—whether pastoral, imprecatory, occasional, doctrinal, or whatever.[14] Of course, this does not mean that the form was ever so fixed as to restrict variations; indeed, there were always so many variations that the very identity of the sermon as a literary form seems at times threatened. If the variations possible within the three main divisions are considered, however, it is evident that Edwards never lost sight of the paradigm.

Text

The Text begins the sermon, invariably with the Scripture passage upon which the formal structure of the sermon rests. Indeed, it is the verse citation of the initial Scripture passage, rather than a word or phrase from the doctrine, that identifies a sermon when it is referred to in Edwards' notebooks. There is no exordium or introduction before the reading of the

---

13. The recovery in the early 1980s of JE's original MS of the *Farewell Sermon* (1750) provided confirmation that, though he employed scrap paper in all late sermons, JE returned to writing out all sermons he considered important.

14. Sermons based upon Old Testament texts tend to have longer Doctrines than those based upon New Testament texts, resulting in some lessening of emphasis upon Application in Old Testament-text sermons. This phenomenon seems to result from a necessity for relating Old Testament materials to the gospel message, which is effected in the Doctrine.

Introduction: Edwards the Preacher

Scripture text, and there need not be any explication or exegesis after it, if the meaning is obvious, in order to have a complete Text. In the vast majority of sermons, however, there is a brief passage (a page, more or less) of comment and explication following the scriptural passage which Edwards designates the Opening of the Text. The Opening consists of several brief, numbered heads, frequently designated "Observation" or "Inference," in which Edwards defines difficult terms, cites other Scripture passages that parallel or complement the textual passage, and generally explains its meaning. In explication, he is never pedantic, even on those rare occasions when he introduces Hebrew or Greek words to clarify definitions; he explains carefully, but does not belabor small points. Indeed, some students of Edwards have felt the Opening of the Text to be the finest part of the sermon because of Edwards' remarkable ability to narrate the statements and events of the text as immediate experience, and in his narrations he not infrequently displays the talent of a first-rate journalist or novelist. But his narrations present concise sketches rather than murals, and the Text is never long.

Doctrine

Following the Text is the Doctrine, a major portion of most sermons and, structurally, often the most complex. The Doctrine usually begins with a single statement of doctrine, carefully labeled "Doc[trine]." In his inclination to formulate the entire doctrinal message of the sermon in a single statement of doctrine, Edwards was, it seems, a little unusual for his day. Most contemporary preachers tended to formulate two or more equally important statements and list them in parallel at the head of the Doctrine. Although it is Edwards' custom to draw two, three, or four Propositions or Observations from the doctrine immediately after its statement, thus dividing it for "clearing" or full discussion in the body of the Doctrine, the single statement of doctrine brings the entire sermon into a sharp thematic focus, like light rays passing through a lens, if only for a vivid moment.

But there need be no formal statement of doctrine at all. Sometimes, when the Scripture text is a clear, concise statement of thesis in itself and in need of no explication, Text and Doctrine elide and the Scripture quotation becomes the statement of doctrine, or, as Edwards puts it, the doctrine is "supplied." At other times, though rarely in Edwards' best days of preaching, there is no statement labeled "Doc[trine]," but only one or two propositions.[15] In such cases, the Proposition differs not at all from the usual statement of doctrine, unless it be a little less assertive in tone.

After the statement of doctrine and the division of the statement into Propositions, Edwards takes up the propositions, explaining the import of each and developing its implications through Inquiries, Observations, Arguments, and plain numbered heads. Each Proposition is also "proved" through Reasons. The term "reason" is actually a generic term for all "proofs" under the Doctrine, and Edwards does not frequently use it as the name for a particular head. The proofs of the doctrine are of two basic types: citations of Scripture (often attended with interpretation), and appeals to human reason and commonplace experience.

Most of the time, particularly in the shorter and middle-length sermons, the Doctrine ends with the giving of various reasons or proofs. However, each Proposition may have its own Use, Improvement, or Application, especially in the longer sermons. This occurs most often when the various propositions have quite different practical implications, and Edwards feels compelled to spell out the different duties implied by each Proposition. However, these uses are within the division of the Doctrine and are not to be confused with the third main division of the sermon. In sermons where such "doctrinal uses" are employed, Edwards often differentiates them from the third main division by calling it the "Application of the Whole."

Application

The Application (or Improvement or Use) is the largest of the three main divisions of the sermon (except in the lecture variant), and in long sermons it may be several times as long as the Text and Doctrine together. It is usually marked by a significant alteration in tone and rhetoric, and by a comparatively simple structure; for whereas the Text and Doctrine are concerned with theory, principle, and precept, the Application is concerned with experience and practice. The Application is directed to specific thoughts, attitudes, and actions of living human beings, and it gives specific advice on these attitudes and actions, in poignant language, in the light of the sermon's doctrine. But as employed by Edwards, the Application also

---

15. A hallmark of the Stockbridge Indian sermons is that, whether written out or in bare outline, they have nothing labeled "Doc[trine]," but only Propositions or Observations, despite being virtual synopses of earlier sermons which had formal statements of doctrine.

Introduction: Edwards the Preacher

has a subtler use as is indicated by his own statement in this transitional passage between the Doctrine and Application of Genesis 19:14.

> The Improvement we shall make of this doctrine shall be to offer some considerations to make future punishment seem real to you.

In effect, then, the Application is a period of hypothetical experience for Edwards' auditory, a time of living imaginatively, through a "willing suspension of disbelief," a series of fictive experiences created and controlled by the preacher.

Uses

The Application or Improvement is generally structured by division into several Uses. Most of the time, the term "use" is restricted to serving as the categorical name for main heads under the division of "Application" or "Improvement," paralleling "reasons" in the Doctrine. (The two division names, incidentally, are used interchangeably, though "Application" appears to be the favored term after the first few years of preaching.) Thus, there is frequently a Use of Self-examination, or a Use of Consolation, and up to four or five such "specialized" uses, though the concluding use is most often the Use of Exhortation. Each Use is subdivided by Inquiries, Considerations, and plain numbered heads, and a list of Considerations or Directions generally concludes the Use of Exhortation.

There are several "paired" heads, such as Objection-Consideration, Enquiry-Answer, and Positive-Negative, that may appear under any one of the three major divisions of the sermon as they are needed, as may such heads as Inference, Observation, or Inquiry. In fact, it should be noted that the minor heads are generally employed in a very flexible way, and are inserted wherever they fit. Few are used only in the Text, Doctrine, or the Application.

In order to have a complete Edwardsean sermon, then, there must be an identifying passage of Scripture at the beginning and an Application (of the whole) at the end; in the middle, there must be a doctrinal discussion of the Bible text, though not necessarily an Opening of the Text or an explicitly labeled "Doc[trine]." The minimal requirements are comparatively easy to describe; the difficulties arise when one attempts to define the "outer limits" of the sermon form.

First, there is the problem of literary form versus pulpit performance. Edwards sometimes speaks of a single preaching session in the pulpit, and that portion of a long sermon which might be preached in one session, as a sermon; but he also speaks of a complex literary unit, which includes several clearly marked preaching units within it, as a sermon. Apparently he was not alone in his ambiguity, for in several eighteenth-century editions his longer sermons are printed as a series of sermons (according to preaching units) rather than as the single long sermons which, according to the form, they are. Such printing conventions preserve the root sense of the Latin *sermo* which means "talk"; moreover, they preserve the spirit of the seventeenth-century New England sermon as a speech act only incidentally preserved in print. When editing his own sermons for the press, however, Edwards scrupulously called sermons of more than one preaching unit "discourses," as in *Discourses on Various Important Subjects*, where some pieces are of one preaching unit and others of more. Modern readers especially must treat the Text-Doctrine-Application unit—however long—as a literary unit: otherwise, they will probably miss theme, logic, and form altogether.

Even when one admits that a sermon may be of any length, as long as it is carefully constructed, without losing its formal unity, there is the complication created by the "paired sermons" and the sermon series. In the case of the paired sermons, Edwards may write two sermons on the same text to be preached in series; however, they share nothing, not even the Opening of the Text, beyond the initial Scripture text. Obviously they are two sermons, though they may, if they are brief, be delivered on the same day. Then there is the variant in which Edwards announces two doctrines in two sermons, but develops only the first doctrine in the first sermon and only the second doctrine in the second sermon. Again, though the sermons are obviously meant to go together, they are formally separated. Such variations, when multiplied, led to the several sermon series which Edwards wrote and preached in the 1730s, including the one presented here.

Obviously, somewhere between the morning-and-afternoon sermon, divided between the Doctrine and the Application so that it could fill the entire Sabbath-day services, and the over-two-hundred-page, thirty-preaching-unit sermon series, the form of the sermon begins to disintegrate. Edwards became a master of his inherited sermon form, but in the 1730s, at the zenith of his mastery, he began experimenting artistically with the sermon. He apparently did everything he could do without actually abandoning the old form entirely, and the only possible conclusion one can draw from the manuscript evidence of his experiments is that he was searching, consciously or unconsciously, for a formal alternative to the sermon itself.

INTRODUCTION
Historical Context

THE SERMONS BY JONATHAN EDWARDS ON THE EPISTLE TO THE Galatians (hereafter "Galatians") were delivered during his pastorate at Northampton. The year following his ordination as assistant pastor, serving together with his maternal grandfather Solomon Stoddard (1643–1729), Edwards preached on Gal. 5:6, which, with its attention to the doctrine and practice of faith resonates with his private notebook on "Faith," begun in January 1728. This sermon, and those on Gal. 2:20 (1728–29) and Gal. 2:17 (1731–32), had been preached prior to the Connecticut Valley revival (ca. 1735–37)—a time in which Edwards became Northampton's sole and senior preacher and established himself as a preacher in New England. However, to follow in his grandfather's footsteps, who "gave a name and reputation" to Northampton, "was no easy matter."[1] In *Faithful Narrative* he recalls,

> Just after my grandfather's death, it seemed to be a time of extraordinary dullness in religion: licentiousness for some years greatly prevailed among the youth of the town; they were many of them very much addicted to night-walking, and frequenting the tavern, and lewd practices, wherein some, by their example exceedingly corrupted others. It was their manner very frequently to get together in conventions of both sexes, for mirth and jollity, which they called frolics; and they would often spend the greater part of the night in them, without regard to any order in the families they

---

1. Cf. George Marsden, *Jonathan Edwards. A Life* (New Haven: Yale University Press, 2003), 125.

belonged to: and indeed family government did too much fail in the town.²

Edwards, however, was winning the approval of the town's parishioners. His father, Timothy Edwards (1669–1758), wrote to Jonathan's sister, Anne Edwards (1699–1790),

> So yt Mr Pierpont tells me ... that ye People of Northampton seem to have a great Love and respect for him, and that they take Great Content in his Ministry. They Continue their usual Kindness to him, and have built him a Good Large Barn ....³

His life, moreover, became busy with travel to New Haven (1729) and Boston (1731), attending the Hampshire Association meeting at Westfield (1731). At this time, he was working on the first entries in the "Blank Bible" (1730) and various "Miscellanies." Also, there was a growing family to support, as daughters Sarah (b. 1728), Jerusha (b. 1730), and Esther (b. 1732) were born.

The sermons on the Galatians of this period contained some major themes Edwards chose to address in Northampton, including justification by faith, spiritual light and sight, human happiness and the glory of God, and the reasonableness of Christianity.⁴ The congregation was not unaffected, as the rise of lay conventicles in the town led to the first awakening during Edwards's ministry at Northampton. He recalled, "And then it was, in the latter part of December [1734], that the Spirit of God began extraordinarily to set in, and wonderfully to work amongst us."⁵ He noticed, too, that the young people were "reforming more and more; they by degrees left off their frolicking, and have been observably more decent in their attendance on the public worship."⁶ Despite, or thanks to, the revival, a "great noise" over Arminianism was noted, as well.⁷

Although the Galatians may have been an antidote to this threat, Edwards's preaching on the epistle is resumed after New England's awakenings. The sermons on Gal. 5:17 (1745), Gal. 3:16 (1746), and Gal. 3:13–14 (1746), were preached after the Great Awakening and leading up to

2. *WJE* 4:146.
3. *WJE* 14:14–15.
4. See for more detail *WJE* 14:17–24.
5. *WJE* 4:149.
6. Edwards writing to Benjamin Colman at Boston on May 30, 1735. See *WJE* 4:99.
7. *WJE* 4:4–18.

the time of his dismissal by the Northampton pastorate. Samuel Hopkins (1721–1803) wrote that "Mr. Edwards was very happy in the esteem and love of his people for many years, and there was the greatest prospect of his living and dying so."[8] The reality was different, as Edwards dealt not only with pastoral issues attempting to keep his young parishioners from "bad books" (i.e., books "to promote lascivious and obscene discourse"),[9] but also publicly stated his thoughts "concerning the qualifications of communicants at the Lord's Table." In fact, his thoughts were opposite to those of his grandfather, which Edwards acknowledged, writing:

> My appearing in this public manner on that side of the question, which is defended in the following sheets, will probably be surprising to many; as 'tis well known, that Mr. Stoddard, so great and eminent a divine, and my venerable predecessor in the pastoral office over the church in Northampton, as well as my own grandfather, publicly and strenuously appeared in opposition to the doctrine here maintained.[10]

To reform the former practice, Edwards appeals to the congregation, preaching in March 1750:

> When he is fully satisfied by searching the Scriptures that his people are going in a way that is wrong-—if in such a case he is as a voice behind them declaring to'em their mistake and saying to 'em, "This is the way: walk in it"-—he does his proper business as a minister of Christ and as the pastor of that church over whom Christ has set him as their teacher and guide in the way of their duty.[11]

However, this and other appeals were of no avail. In June 1750, the male voting members overwhelmingly voted for his dismission.[12]

Although dismissed by the Northampton church, Edwards stayed in touch with his former congregants. The sermon on Gal. 5:6 highlights his

---

8. Samuel Hopkins, *The Life and character of the late Reverend Jonathan Edwards, President of the College of New Jersey : together with a number of his sermons on various important subjects* (Boston: S. Kneeland, 1765), 53.

9. Hopkins, *The Life and character*, 53–54.

10. *WJE* 12:167, An Humble Inquiry into the Rules of the Word of God, Concerning the Qualifications Requisite to a Complete Standing and Full Communion in the Visible Christian Church (1749).

11. *WJE* 25:448.

12. Hopkins, *The Life and character*, 61.

return visits, not to his old pulpit, but to meetings in private houses of his supporters. This sermon was preached in March 1751 in Pascommuck, a small hamlet south of Northampton, at the home of Noah Clark. Edwards had lent "Rector Wms Seasonable Plea" to Clark (1694–1776), and he had received books from this parishioner and deacon.[13] As was his habit with many of his sermons, the sermon on Gal. 5:6 was repreached, this one in January 1752, possibly at Stockbridge.

The sermons on the Galatians, then, were preached in the period prior to and following the Connecticut Valley and New England awakenings. That is not to say that Edwards did not reflect on this epistle at other times in his life. One has merely to look at the references to Galatians in the "Miscellanies," *Religious Affections* (1746), the sermons on 1 Cor. 13 (1738) published as *Charity and its Fruits*, "Notes on Scripture" (ca. 1729–57), and other writings in the period of the late 1730s and early 1740s to see that this epistle was of consistent interest to Edwards. In fact, his various reflections on Galatians fall into a longstanding Christian tradition of biblical exegesis and exposition.

Early modern New England was the recipient of the commentaries, treatises, and homilies on the Galatians written prior to Edwards, such as works of Guilielmus Estius (1542–1613), Wolfgang Musculus (1497–1563), David Pareus (1548–1622), and William Perkins (1558–1602), among others. In fact, the libraries of the colleges of Harvard and Yale,[14] as well as private collections of the pastors of the British colony,

---

13. Elisha Williams, *The essential rights and liberties of Protestants. A seasonable plea for the liberty of conscience, and the right of private judgment, in matters of religion, without any controul from human authority. Being a letter, from a gentleman in the Massachusetts-Bay to his friend in Connecticut. Wherein some thoughts on the origin, end, and extent of the civil power, with brief considerations on several late laws in Connecticut, are humbly offered* (Boston: S. Kneeland and T. Green in Queenstreet, 1744). Cf. 26:27. On receiving books see *WJE* 16:87. On objectors to the dismissal of Edwards, see *WJE* 38, "Notes for the Petition of the Northampton Minority, [c. 1751]"; and Jennifer McCleery, "A Profile of the Northampton Minority," *Jonathan Edwards Studies* 7, no. 1 (2017).

14. See, for example, *A Catalogue of the Library of Yale College in New Haven* (New London: T. Green, 1743), 23 ("V. Annotations on the Bible"), 24 ("Estius in Epistolas Pauli"; "Pareus on Gal."); 39–40 (Patristic commentaries and opera); *Catalogus Librorum Bibliothecae Collegij Harvardini quod est Cantabrigiae in Nova Anglia* (Boston: B. Green, 1723), 4 ("Biblia Polygotta"); 8 ("Cyril of Alexandria, *Opera Omnia*"; "Chrystostom, *Operum Omnium*"); 13 ("Erasmus, Paraphrase on the N. Testament"), 14 ("Gregory of Nyssa, *Opera*"; "Rodolph Gualteri, *Homiliæ in Pauli Epist. Ad Galatas*"), 17 ("Hieronimus, *Operum*"); 20 ("Cornelius À Lapide, *Comment. in Pauli Epistolas*"; "Martin Luther, *Operum*"), 23 ("Wolfgang Musculus, *Comment. In Pauli Epistolas*"), 24 ("Gregory of Nazianzus,

contained many of the works of the past, including interpretative reflections on Galatians.¹⁵ In that regard, the library of Edwards' father, Timothy Edwards (1669-1758), and Edwards' own book collection were less representative, though the following works are noted: Locke's *A Paraphrase and Notes on the Epistle of St. Paul to the Galatians*, Poole's *Synopsis criticorum*, and *A Plea for ye Ministers of ye Gospel, offered to the consideration of the people of New-England: Being an exposition of Galat. VI. 6*.¹⁶ Furthermore, Edwards' exegetical reflections on Galatians did not only come down from the pulpit but are also found in private notes, such as the "Blank Bible," "Notes on Scripture," and references are to be found in published and unpublished works.¹⁷

Finally, the Protestant Reformation found Galatians a source for the formulation of Protestant doctrines of such loci as Christology, redemption, and faith, recurring themes of *continuity* in the sermons of Edwards on Galatians. Yet, at the same time, the seeming *discontinuity* of these surviving sermons in regard to the doctrine of justification, for example, famously present in the sermons and commentary of Martin Luther (1483-1546), cannot go unnoticed.

Opera"); 25 ("Poole, Matth., *Synopsis Crit.*"), 26 ("William Perkins, *Works* (3 vols)"; "David Pareus, *Operum Theologicorum Exegeticorum*"), 50 ("Luther (Mart.), *Commentary on Galatians*"), 56 ("William Perkins, *Exposition on the Chapters of Galatians*"), 64 ("Geor. Weinrichii, *Comment. in Eph. Galat.*)"; 80 ("Hugo Grotius, *Epistolæ ad Gallos*").

15. For private libraries see, for example, *A catalogue of curious and valuable books, belonging to the late reverend & learned, Mr. Ebenezer Pemberton* (Boston: B. Green, 1717), 1 ("Poli, *Synopsis*"), 4 ("Greg. Nazianzus, *Opera*"); *A catalogue of rare and valuable books, being the greatest part of the library of the late Reverend and learned, Mr. Joshua Moodey* (Boston: S. Kneeland, 1718), 4 ("H. Bullengeri, *Comment. in omnes Apostol. Epistolas*"), 8 ("Calvini, *Comment. in Epist. Ad Gal.*"), 11 ("D. Parei, *Comment. in Epost. Ad Galatas*"); and *A catalogue of curious and valuable books, being the greatest part of the libraries of the Reverend and learned Mr. Rowland Cotton* (Boston: Samuel Gerrish Bookseller, 1725), 3 ("Anselmus in *Omnes Pauli Epist.*"; "Greg. Nazianzeni, *Opera*"), 7 ("Luther's *Commentary on Galatians*"), 13 ("Lutheri in *Epist. Pauli ad Galat. Comment.*")

16. See further, *WJE* 26.

17. See for example, on Gal. 5:6a, *WJE* 8:139, 140, 299; *WJE* 21:473; *WJE* 24:532, 1085, 1173, and *WJE* 25:525; on Gal. 2:20, *WJE* 2:168, 491 (*Religious Affections*); *WJE* 7:512 (*The Life of David Brainerd*); *WJE* 8:141 (sermon one, "Charity and Its Fruits"); *WJE* 16:200 (Letter to the Rev. Stephen Williams, 1746); *WJE* 17:281, *WJE* 18:534; *WJE* 19:207; *WJE* 19:479; *WJE* 27 "Controversies" Notebook; on Gal. 2:17, *WJE* 18:102; *WJE* 23:183, and *WJE* 24:1080; on Gal. 5:17, *WJE* 8:389; *WJE* 18:143, 234; *WJE* 21:192; *WJE* 24:927, 1008, 1038, 1067, 1085–1090, and 1180; on Gal. 3:16 *WJE* 21:109–44, 145–48; *WJE* 24:138, 1081–82; on Gal. 3:13, *WJE* 2:236.

Sermons on the Epistle to the Galatians

ONLY THAT SORT OF FAITH THAT WORKS BY LOVE AVAILS ANYTHING BEFORE GOD

(Gal. 5:6, 1728)

THE RELATION OF FAITH AND WORKS IN THE *ORDU SALUTIS* IS ONE THAT preoccupied theologians long before Edwards, but he too grappled with it, particularly in the context of the emerging revivalistic culture of early eighteenth-century Anglo-America. Here, in a sermon from early 1728, he focuses on the "faith that worketh by love," exploring the meanings of love both in the individual and in the divine.

This sermon, preached in the winter of 1728, on the nature of saving and justifying faith, appears to be the culmination of much consideration on the topic. Beginning in 1722, Edwards recorded numerous definitions and reflections upon the subject of faith and the centrality of love to such faith.[1]

There are three important features to this sermon. In the first place, Edwards shows his commitment to covenant theology in his regular utilization of the dichotomy of the covenants of works and grace. To seek justification according to faith is to live under the new covenant or covenant of grace, whereas to seek to find acceptance before God by any other means is to live under the covenant of works.

Second, Edwards spends the vast majority of the sermon defining and describing true faith. Here he demonstrates his Reformed pedigree.

---

1. See for example, The "Miscellanies" in *WJE* 13:33, 37, 212, 216, 218–19, 244–45, 254, 256, 299, and 329.

Only that Sort of Faith that Works by Love Avails Anything before God

His definition of faith as "the heart's receiving of Christ and his gospel," sounds strikingly similar to that of William Ames, who defined it as "the resting of the heart on God (*fides est acquiescentia cordis in Deo*).[2] Edwards' description betrays an unmistakably Amesian influence. However, Edwards' more Christological focus emerges from the comparison of definitions. Likewise, in keeping with the Reformation and post-Reformation discussions on the nature of faith, Edwards distinguishes between three elements or "orders" to "true faith": assent, consent, and trust (*assentia, notitia,* and *fiducia*). In these ways, Edwards demonstrates in this sermon, the influence of continental Reformed theology upon his thinking, especially that of Ames.

One way that we can tell when an issue is important for Edwards as a pastor and preacher is by the length and complexity of his Exposition, and here he provides a detailed explication of the early verses of Galatians 5, and of his text, v. 6, showing how justification is indeed by faith and not by any works of law, such as circumcision. But what is faith? He commences the Doctrine with a definition, drawing on his new notebook on "Faith," at the time of this sermon containing only the first twenty or so entries. Faith, Edwards summarizes, is receiving Christ and his gospel. "Receiving" entails not merely a recognition of faith but an assent of the heart, or of the will, a change in disposition. In true faith, there is an assent of the soul in believing the gospel, as it has the "image of God"; a consent of the mind to what is offered in the gospel (salvation through Christ); and trust in Christ as Savior, including counting on Christ for happiness and deliverance, being content in Christ's promises, and venturing one's interest in a dependence on Christ. Secondly, only an "efficacious, working faith" avails with God. Faith is an assent of the heart, but true faith is manifested in proper fruits, or out-workings of love. "Man is justified by faith alone," Edwards states, "but not only that faith that is alone." Finally, good works that flow out from this faith are by love: love to Christ, love to fellow Christians. In fact, this theme, in connection with Galatians 5:6, is repeated by Edwards in sermons from the winter of 1728 till after his dismissal in July 1750, as in "Charity and Its Fruits," a notebook entitled "Signs of Godliness," and the "Blank Bible."[3]

---

2. See William Ames, *Medulla Theologica* (1634), I.iii.1.
3. *WJE* 8:139, 140, 299; *WJE* 21:473; *WJE* 24:532, 1085, 1173, and *WJE* 25:525.

Finally, the Application of this sermon is filled with urgent appeals to the heart and emotions in a way that appears much stronger than his Applications in later sermons. The final paragraphs are filled with probing questions meant to move his hearers and, clearly, to stir their affections. For example, he asks, "Did you come to Christ . . . and give yourself to Christ with your whole heart? Did you ever *feel* your heart willing you [to] do any such thing as this, or do you now *feel* it? . . . Is God's method of saving sinners by mere [grace], for the sake of the worthiness of his Son, what you *feel* your heart join with? Does that seem the pleasantness and most delightsome way of being saved, of any way that you can think of?" Such appeals were conspicuously absent when he preached a different sermon on this text in Galatians in 1752 (*Saving Faith Worketh by Love*, below). Perhaps the timing of the sermon accounts for the difference. Edwards preached this early iteration on the text several years prior to the revivals, while the latter was delivered in 1751, after the revivals and the publication of *Religious Affections* (1746), and, perhaps more to the point, after his bitter dismissal from Northampton. Perhaps the enthusiastic and emotional extravagances of the awakenings produced greater caution in Edwards' preaching, particularly in the utilization of emotional exhortations.

The Application, then, is an extended interrogation, providing questions and methods for the listeners to examine their souls to see if they have true faith. Edwards first gives no less than nine specific directions on how to "try" oneself, or examine one's soul. He then goes on to query whether the faith his congregants have is one that shows faith by works, that is built not on fear but love, and that obeys God's commands and is not hypocritical. He concludes with a series of "considerations" as a way to inspire his people to seek this faith: consider its excellency, its pleasantness, usefulness, equity and reasonableness, and its absolute necessity.

The sermon illustrates, finally, an interpretative continuity with past exegetes. This essential understanding of the text's words resonates, for example, with Luther's commentary on the Galatians on the same text:

> Paul therefore in this place setteth forth the whole life of a Christian (*totam vitam Christianam*), namely, that inwardly it consiseth in faith towards God, and outwardly in charity and good works towards our neighbour. So that a man is a perfect Christian inwardly through faith before God, who hath no need of our works,

Only that Sort of Faith that Works by Love Avails Anything before God

and outwardly before men, whom our faith profiteth nothing, but our charity or our works.[4]

And so, William Perkins echoes Luther's reading of the text:

The meaning of the text is, that faith is effectuall in it selfe: and that it shewes and puts forth his efficacie by loue, as by the fruit thereof. And it cannot hence be gathered, that faith is acted and mooued by loue as by a formall cause.[5]

Furthermore, Matthew Poole, in *Annotations Upon the Holy Bible*, commented, "Faith is not an idle, inactive, inoperative Faith; but such a Faith as worketh by love towards God and towards men."[6] Matthew Henry, in *An Exposition of the Old and New Testament*, concurred that it is "such a faith in Christ as discovers itself to be true and genuine, by a sincere love to God and our neighbour."[7] Noteworthy is that John Locke, in *A Paraphrase and Notes on the Epistles of St. Paul to the Galatians*, a work also familiar to Edwards, deviates from the consensus of interpretation, paraphrasing the text as "all that is available is faith alone, working by love."[8]

* * * * *

The manuscript is thirteen duodecimo leaves. Edwards' shorthand notation at the top of the first page indicates that the sermon was "preached a second time" at an unspecified place, apparently from a passage in Luke. The Northampton symbol appears several lines down, immediately after the text.

---

4. Martin Luther, *Commentary upon the Epistle to the Galatians: abridged, without any alterations* . . . (London: J. Brotherton and J. Oswald, 1734), 192–93.

5. William Perkins, *A commentarie or exposition, vpon the fiue first chapters of the Epistle to the Galatians: penned by the godly, learned, and iudiciall diuine, Mr. W. Perkins. Now published for the benefit of the Church, and continued with a supplement vpon the sixt chapter, by Rafe Cudworth Bachelour of Diuinitie* ([Cambridge]: Iohn Legat, printer to the Vniuersitie of Cambridge, 1604), 383.

6. Matthew Poole, *Annotations Upon the Holy Bible* (London: Thomas Parkhurst et al., 1700), vol. II, Galatians V:6.

7. Matthew Henry, *An Exposition of the Old and New Testament* (Philadelphia: Ed. Barrington & Geo. D. Haswell, 1828), VI:528.

8. John Locke, *A Paraphrase and Notes on the Epistles of St. Paul to the Galatians* (London: Printed for Thomas Tegg et al., 1823), 62.

Only that Sort of Faith that Works by Love Avails Anything before God

GALATIANS 5:6

For in Jesus Christ neither circumcision availeth anything, nor uncircumcision; but faith that worketh by love.

It seems that there were some false teachers risen up, that had been amongst the Galatians, endeavoring to instill into them that it was necessary, in order to their justification and salvation, that they should conform to the legal observances and rites of the law of Moses, and particularly that they should be circumcised.

This doctrine, tending to make the grace of God in Christ none effect, and overthrowing the sufficiency of Jesus Christ for salvation, and being directly contrary to that great doctrine of the gospel, justification by faith, the Apostle writes this epistle to them, to bring them off from those principles, and insists very much upon the contrary doctrine of justification only by faith, and upon the uselessness of the works of the law to that end, and the danger of depending on legal performances.

And in this chapter, he is upon the same argument. "Stand fast," says he in the 1st verse, "in the liberty wherewith Christ hath made us free, and be not entangled again with the yoke of bondage"; that is, "Resolutely maintain the liberty which Christ has given us from the burdensome legal services, and your liberty from the covenant of works, that you may not be obliged by that either perfectly to obey the law, or else to suffer the penalty of it."

Only that Sort of Faith that Works by Love Avails Anything before God

"Behold, I Paul," says he in the 2nd verse, "say unto you, if ye be circumcised, Christ shall profit you nothing"; [i.e.,] "If you think circumcision is necessary in order to your justification, and that the gospel of Jesus Christ is not sufficient without it, and have a dependence upon that partly to justify you, Christ will profit you nothing; you'll receive no benefit by him whom you think not sufficient alone for your salvation."

He goes on in the 3rd verse: "For I testify unto every man that is circumcised, that he is a debtor to the whole law"; that is, by seeking to be justified by that or any other work, he puts himself under the covenant of works, and is a debtor either to bring forth perfect obedience, or to suffer the penalty of the law.

"For Christ" (as he goes on in the 4th verse) "is become of no effect to you, whosoever of you are justified by the law; ye are fallen from grace." [I.e.,] "Seeing ye have dependence upon works, you have nothing to do with free grace, nor will you have any benefit by that which you have no dependence upon."

"For," says the Apostle in the 5th verse, "we through the Spirit wait for the hope of righteousness through faith." Though we that are Christians don't expect salvation by the works of the law—for that is not the profession of Christians—but by faith wrought not by ourselves, but by the Spirit.

And then come in the words of the text: "For in Jesus Christ neither circumcision availeth anything, nor uncircum[cision]; but faith that worketh by love."

"In Jesus Christ": that is, amongst us Christians, those that are under the gospel, under the second covenant.

"Neither circumcision nor uncircumcision availeth anything": that is, it signifies nothing before God, in the business of justification, to be circumcised or not circumcised, or to do or not to do any other legal performances.

But only faith in Jesus Christ, "that works by love": not any sort of faith, not a barren and fruitless faith, but one that is fruitful in a holy life; not a faith that is alone, but a faith that is accompanied by love, and that acts and produces good works by it.

The words may be translated, "faith which is wrought" or "perfected by love"; but then the sense would not be very different. The apostle James says, in the 2nd chapter of his epistle, at the 22nd verse, in the former part of the verse, "faith wrought with works"; and in the latter, that "by works faith was made perfect." That is, the perfection and truth of it consists in that, that it is a working faith; the same in substance is signified by both expressions.

DOCTRINE

Only that sort of faith that works by love avails anything before God.

In speaking to this Doctrine, we shall do these three things:

I. We shall show what faith is.

II. [Show] that 'tis only an efficacious, working faith that avails anything before [God].

III. [Show] that the works that true faith produces, are the exercises and fruits of love.

But in the

I. [First] place, we shall explain what faith is. Which I shall do for these ends: [first,] because a great many persons have but a very poor notion what faith is. They hear that we must believe and that we must trust in Christ for salvation, but they don't know what it is to believe, what it is to trust; don't know the meaning of those words when used in this case, and so they don't know what it is they are to seek and pray for. And then another end, is that persons may be satisfied concerning themselves, that when they distinctly know what faith is, they may judge whether or no they have [it].

Therefore, [faith] may be defined, in the general, thus:

Faith is the heart's receiving of Christ and his gospel.[1] 'Tis easy to understand what we mean by the heart's receiving a thing: there is an outward receiving, and there is a receiving of the mind and heart. A person may receive a thing, and yet his heart not receive it. A woman that is sought in marriage may, for certain reasons, receive her lover, when her heart don't receive him. A child that is adopted may, for certain reasons, receive his adopting father, when his heart don't receive him; his heart don't close with the offer he makes of being his father.

Believing in [Christ] is a receiving of Christ, as is plain from John 1:12, "But as many as received him, to them gave he power to become the

---

1. This sermon was written in early 1728, at the very time that JE began his notebook on "Faith." This definition here repeats and merges some of his definitions in entries 1–20 (*WJE* 21:417–20).

sons of God, even to them that believe on his name." Where the Evangelist tells what he means by receiving him: even believing on his name.

This receiving is a receiving of the heart. Faith is an act of the heart. Rom. 10:10, "For with the heart man believeth unto righteousness; and with the mouth confession is made unto salvation." The door that Christ stands at, and knocks and calls for entrance, is the door of the heart. Man looks at the outward appearance, but God looks at the heart. That is the call of Christ, Prov. 23:26, "My son, give me thine heart"; and every believer, in believing, gives Jesus Christ his heart.

In faith, the heart receives Christ and his gospel. The gospel of Jesus Christ is that declaration which he makes of the wonderful grace of God in his readiness to pardon, sanctify and receive into his favor, and to bestow eternal life upon all sinners for Christ's sake and through his righteousness, and the offer of pardon, sanctification and salvation in this method, and the offer Christ makes of himself to all. The heart of a believer receives and gives entertainment to this gospel: his heart closes with Christ's salvation, which is a salvation from punishment and from sin, a giving a life of happiness and of holiness; his heart closes with his way of salvation by mere grace, through the worthiness and righteousness of Christ; his heart accepts the offer of being Christ's, of being his disciple, his servant and his spouse. The gospel is a gospel to him. The meaning of the word "gospel," is "glad tidings"; it is glad tidings to his heart to hear that God is willing, of his wonderful grace, to accept and save poor sinners through Christ. He believes it, and it rejoices his heart, not only because he may be saved, but because he may be saved through Christ.

In order to true faith, there must be the assent of the soul, and its consent and trust or reliance.

First. There must be the assent of the soul in believing the truth of the gospel: a believing that Christ is the Son of God; a believing the sufficiency of Christ for our salvation to deliver from sin and all misery, and make us completely blessed; a believing that God is willing to accept and pardon and bestow eternal life upon his account, and that he certainly will do it to those [that] believe that he will surely perform his promises. 'Tis not a guess or a mere opinion, as men have their several opinions about doubtful things, but a being fully persuaded. Rom. 4:20–21, "He staggered not at the promise of God through unbelief; but was strong in faith, giving glory to God; and being fully persuaded that, what he had promised, he was able also to perform." John 6:69, "we know and are sure that thou art the Christ, the Son of the living God."

Now this persuasion of the truth of the gospel, arises from that image and glory of God which he sees in the gospel. He sees in the gospel that majesty, that wisdom, that holiness, that beauty and excellency, that grace, and feels that power which makes up the idea of God, and makes him sure and confident that it comes from a Being that has that majesty, wisdom, holiness, power, excellency and grace in himself. He sees and feels divinity in the gospel, and that makes him sure that it comes from one that is divine.

When we converse with a man, and see his countenance and gestures, and hear him talk, we are convinced that those sounds, and those gestures and that air of countenance, proceeds from something within him that has understanding and will. So there is as much appearance of a divine understanding, wisdom, holiness, majesty and grace in the Word of God, as there is of a human understanding in the countenance, voice and gesture of a rational man.

Now God opens the understanding of a believer to see this. He does as it were see God's countenance in his Word; he sees those marks of excellency and glory that are peculiar to God. He is satisfied that it came from God, because he sees God in it. This testimony which God gives a believer of the truth of the gospel, is what the apostle John seems to speak [of]. [I] John 5:10, "He that believeth on the Son of God hath the witness in himself."

Second. There is the consent of the mind to what is proposed and offered in the gospel. Christ offers himself, and offers that eternal life which he has purchased. He offers himself to be this guide, this intercessor, this Lord and Savior; and the believer's heart consents. This is that act more especially whereby Christ becomes our Savior, and whereby we are justified. 'Tis the act of the will and of the inclination of the mind. The soul is drawn to Christ Jesus; the heart in its inclination and disposition, which before was opposite, now yields and closes with Christ and his salvation. He feels his natural disposition to be towards Christ; he highly prizes and esteems him. He is sweet and pleasant to his soul. He delights in the gospel, he relishes the glorious truths of it; they suit his inward disposition.

He chooses Jesus Christ to be his Lord and Savior. He chooses him above any other, chooses him freely. When I say "freely," I mean without being brought to it by fear, or merely an aim at any private benefit. He

Only that Sort of Faith that Works by Love Avails Anything before God

chooses him for his own sake. And he also chooses his way of salvation above all others: it suits him better to be saved by mere grace, by the love of Christ and for his worthiness, than to be saved any other way.

To be thus, is to be truly willing that Christ should be our Savior. 'Tis for want of this, that men miss of salvation. Matt. 23:37, "how often would I have gathered thy children together, as a hen gathereth her chickens under her wings, and ye would not!" John 5:40, "And ye will not come unto me, that ye might have life."

Third. There must be a trust, a reliance upon Jesus Christ as our Mediator and Savior. Eph. 1:12, "That we should be to the praise of his glory, who first trusted in Christ"; that is, who were first believers. To believe Christ, is to believe what he declares and promises to us. To believe in Christ, is to trust in him. To have faith in any person, is to put confidence in him.

Now that you may fully understand what is meant by trusting in Christ, you may take notice that there are these three things signified by it:

1. A looking to Christ, as being he in whom is our happiness, and an expecting of it through him, and him only; a looking to him only for deliverance from sin and misery, and for the communication of life and happiness. The word "trust" is sometimes used in Scripture for the expecting of happiness from a thing. Mark 10:24, "how hard is it for them that trust in riches to enter into the kingdom of God"; that is, that expect happiness from their riches, and set their hearts upon them as their portion. So it seems to be used, Ezek. 16:15, "But thou didst trust in thy beauty."

True believers, they look for happiness and salvation only from and in Jesus Christ. Indeed, they look upon him as their happiness, as their pearl of great price. This is called "looking" to Christ. Is. 45:22, "Look unto me all ye ends of the earth, and be ye saved." This was represented by looking to the brazen serpent in the wilderness [Num. 21:8–9].

2. By trusting in Christ, is meant the soul's resting and being easy and satisfied in the belief of the promises made in him. If we say that we put confidence in anyone for the fulfillment of his promises, we mean that our mind is easy and rests satisfied in a belief that he will perform them. If we say a man trusts in a castle or fort to defend him from his enemies, we mean that he rests and is quiet in that belief, that the castle is sufficient to defend him.

3. To trust in Christ, is to venture our whole interest in a dependence upon his salvation. To do thus, is to cast ourselves upon him, to deliver ourselves up to him and venture ourselves upon him. He that durst not venture his all upon Christ, don't put full confidence in him; he durst not trust him so far as that comes to.

But he that truly trusts in Christ, will venture to forego and miss of every other enjoyment in a dependence upon that that is better from him. He'll venture his ease and he'll venture his pleasure, he'll venture his worldly profit and he'll venture his honor and his friends, yea, and his own life, and is ready to miss of or lose any of these things, if they stand in the way of Christ, his following him or his being found in him. Luke 14:26–27, "If any man come to me, and hate not his father, and mother, and wife, and children, yea, and his own life also, he cannot be my disciple. And whosoever doth not bear his cross, and come after me, he cannot be my disciple."

Every believer has such a dependence upon happiness from Christ, that he does forego and utterly cast away all sinful ways of procuring his own pleasure, as by sensuality or worldliness, and is ready to cast away every enjoyment in itself lawful, if it should not consent with his profession of religion or obedience to God.

II. 'Tis only an efficacious, working faith that avails anything before God. By "an efficacious, working faith," we mean that that does the proper work of faith in the heart, and brings forth the proper fruits of it in the life.

There is a faith that is lifeless, barren and ineffectual, makes no great or lasting alteration in the heart or life.

The proper work of faith in the heart, is to change and renew the heart, to work a new nature, to take off the heart and affections from earthly things and to make them heavenly, to make the heart holy, humble, patient, submissive, meek, charitable. Such a disposition as this, is the natural, genuine work of true Christian faith, and this is what an effectual faith will produce. Gala. 5:22–23, "But the fruit of the Spirit is love, joy, peace, longsuffering, gentleness, goodness, faith, meekness, temperance."

The work of faith in the life, is to make the person in whom it is, to be exceeding careful to keep all the commandments of God, desirous to know what their duty is and ready to do it, afraid to do anything that shall be displeasing to God. It makes persons live in the exercise of a tender conscience, to live lives of purity, lives of temperance, lives of righteousness and charitableness, lives of prayer and lives of thankfulness to God for his mercy.

That faith that don't bear such fruits and produce such good works as these, is a dead faith: for if it were alive, it [would] bear fruit. They that say they have faith, and don't bring forth such like good works, are like the dry limbs of a tree that must be lopped off. John 15:2, "Every branch in me that beareth not fruit he taketh away."

A man can't reasonably suppose that he believes in Christ, if he don't thus live such a life. I John, 2nd chapter, 3rd and 4th verses: "hereby we do know that we know him, if we keep his commandments. He that saith, I know him, and keepeth not his commandments, is a liar, and the truth is not in him."

Faith alone, without those works, won't justify. Man is justified by faith alone, but not by that faith that is alone; that is, 'tis only his faith that has influence in the matter of justification, but always that faith that is accompanied by works. Jas. 2:14, "What doth it profit, my brethren, though a man say he hath faith, and have not works? can faith save him?" And in the 18th verse, "Yea, a man may say, Thou hast faith, and I have works: show me thy faith without thy works, and I will show thee my faith by my works."

III. Those good works which faith produces are by love, or do flow from love. Evangelical obedience flows from love, and not principally from fear. True believers do the will of God freely, not because they are forced by threatenings and the rod; they ben't drove, but drawn. The obedience of a saint is a "labor of love," Heb. 6:10. 'Tis the obedience of children arising from dutifulness, love and reverence, and not the obedience of slaves. Rom. 8:14–15, "For as many as are led by the Spirit of God, are the sons of God. For ye have not received the spirit of bondage again unto fear; but ye have received the Spirit of adoption, whereby ye cry, Abba, Father."

There is none of our obedience is good for anything without love, as the Apostle plainly tells us. I Cor. 13:3, "though I bestow all my goods to feed the poor, and though I give my body to be burned, and have not charity, it profiteth me nothing." By "charity" is meant not only love to men, but love to God, as any may be satisfied by looking upon the three first verses of the 8th [chapter] of I Corinthians.

Those dispositions of heart and those fruits of life, are the natural fruit of love. As in the same 13th of Corinthians, 4th, 5th, 6th and 7th verses: "Charity suffereth long, and is kind; charity envieth not; charity vaunteth not itself, is not puffed up, doth not behave itself unseemly, seeketh not her own, is not easily provoked, thinketh no evil; rejoices not in iniquity, but rejoiceth in the truth; beareth all things, believeth all things, hopeth all things. endureth all things."

The love that faith works by, is twofold:

First. Love to Christ. Herein, I would not exclude love to God the Father: for in loving the Son, we love the Father. The true believer, he loves the Lord Jesus Christ above all; he has chosen him for his best beloved, his nearest friend and his highest happiness; he sees a purity and ravishing excellency in him, that powerfully draws forth his love to him.

Second. Love to Christians, for Christ's sake. This is a great part of Christian holiness, as is evident by its being so much insisted on and so much set by in the Word of [God], and is given as the distinguishing mark of a Christian, whereby others may know us, and we know ourselves. 'Tis given as a mark whereby others may know us. John 13:35, "Hereby shall all men know that ye are my disciples, if ye have love one to another." And it's given as a mark, whereby we may know ourselves. [I] John 3:14, "we know that we are passed from death to life, because we love the brethren." The apostle James speaks of works of this kind as the proper fruits by which faith is known, Jas. 2:15–16.

APPLICATION

And,

First. In this Doctrine, there is a great deal of foundation laid for the trying of ourselves. There is no need of repeating of those things that have been mentioned for you to examine yourself by, if you went along with what has been said, and tried yourself by it as it was delivered. But however, it may be of use more particularly to apply those things by way of examination. Therefore, inquire of yourself:

1. Did your heart ever receive Christ Jesus, and give entertainment to the gospel? Did you come to Christ, accept of Christ and give yourself to Christ with your whole heart? Did you ever feel your heart willing you [to] do any such thing as this, or do you now feel it? Is God's method of saving sinners by mere [grace], for the sake of the worthiness of his Son, what you feel your heart join with? Does that seem the pleasantest and most delightsome way of being saved, of any way that you can think of?

2. Are you fully persuaded of the truth of the gospel because you see God in it? You see that glory, that excellency, that wisdom and beauty in it that convinces ye, that convinces you that it comes from God, that it is certainly the word of the everlasting God.

3. Did you ever freely choose Jesus Christ to be your Lord and your Savior? Did you choose him for his own sake, because you saw him worthy to be chosen, without being driven to it by fear of punishment, or brought to it merely by any private view at your own safety and preservation from misery?

4. Does your inclination agree with the gospel? Do you naturally incline to Jesus Christ? Does his salvation suit your natural inclination? Do you savor and relish those things that are exhibited in the gospel?

5. Do you look for your happiness only by Jesus Christ? All men are seeking their own happiness: some look for it in worldly things, some look for it in honor, some in riches, some in friends. But do you look for happiness in Jesus Christ?

6. Does your mind rest in that expectation? Are you easy and satisfied in the dependence you have upon Christ for happiness and eternal life?

7. Do you venture your whole interest in your dependence upon Christ? Do you forego unlawful pleasures and profits, and deny yourself for him, and are you ready to [be] forgoing all other things for him, if you should be called to it?

8. Is your faith a working faith? Does [it] change your heart and give you a principle of new life, make you to be of that Christian temper and disposition which you have heard described? And does it make you to live a pure, holy and heavenly life, make you conscientiously and carefully obedient to all God's commands? And,

[9.] Lastly, does your obedience flow from love, a hearty and sincere love to Jesus Christ and to God's people, for Christ's sake? Is your obedience a labor of love? Is it the obedience of a child, that arises from love and dutifulness towards your father and brotherly kindness towards your brethren, or is it only the obedience of a slave, that is drove to his work by fear?

If you are sure that you find one these, you may be sure that you have them all. Any one of 'em, if it be really in you, is that which will never fail, and may assure you that you are passed from death to life.

Therefore, be exceeding careful in examining of yourself, and watch that you don't content yourself with a listless and fruitless faith. And always remember that nothing is of any avail before God, but faith that works by love.

Secondly. We learn by this Doctrine, that although 'tis only faith without works that justifies, yet that Christian religion secures obedience and good works. There is no room left for any one to say that they have faith which justifies, and that they need take no care about works, and so to give themselves a liberty in sinning because they ben't under the law, but under grace. For though 'tis only faith that justifies, yet there is no faith that justifies but a working faith. So that it is as impossible that any person should be saved without works, as if they were justified upon the account of their works. It is as impossible that man should be saved without an evangelical, universal and sincere obedience under the second covenant, as[2] it was that they should be saved without a perfect obedience under the first covenant.

Thirdly. The new covenant lays a foundation for a better obedience, than would be laid if the condition of it were the works of the law: for the covenant being free, the offer of eternal life being made upon Christ's account, and not upon our own obedience, is free also. Fear of hell is taken away by Christ, so that the obedience of a Christian don't arise from a slavish fear, but from love.

If works were the condition of eternal life, there would be a great deal more probability of men's obedience being merely mercenary, and purely from respect to self, and not from a gracious respect to God and Jesus Christ.

Fourthly. Those that ben't careful to obey God's commands because they think they are converted, may by this Doctrine be convicted of their hypocrisy. If they had faith, it would more careful to do their duty, for that is one work of a living, working faith: to make men conscientious and very careful that they don't offend God, nor do that which shall be displeasing to him, and that, because, as a child, they reverence, love and stand in awe of God their Father.

Fifthly. Let those that have not this faith, be exhorted earnestly to seek it and pray for it. And to stir you up so to do, consider:

---

2. MS: "and."

Only that Sort of Faith that Works by Love Avails Anything before God

1. The excellency of it. Faith in Jesus Christ is so excellent a thing, that the Apostle counted all things as loss and dung for the excellency of it. The excellency appears in the fountain of it, which is God's eternal, electing love; and from the object of it, which is not only the precious promises of God's Word, but God himself and an all-sufficient Mediator. And from the effects of it: for it ennobles the believer's person, his nature, his prayers, his works, his state and condition; it makes men the servants, the friends and the sons of God, and the brethren, the members and the beloved and the espoused of Jesus Christ.

2. The pleasantness of it. It many ways eases, calms and quiets the mind. It comforts it in adversity, and fills with joy unspeakable. It gives experience of the lovingkindness of God, and begets a joyful hope of eternal rest. Matt. 11:28, "Come unto all ye that labor and are heavy laden, and I will give you rest." Is. 55:1–2, "come ye, and buy wine and milk without money and without price. [. . .] Eat ye that which is good, and let your soul delight itself in fatness."

3. The usefulness [of it]. It gives new life to the dead soul. It begins in the soul eternal life. It is the bond of union with Jesus Christ, and the foundation of communion with him. It procures justification, adoption and glorification. It supplies the believer with invincible strength, whereby he overcomes the world, overcomes Satan and his lusts, overcomes the greatest calamities, overcomes death itself, yea, overcomes God. Gen. 32:28, "for as a prince thou hast power with God, and hast prevailed."

4. The equity and reasonableness of it. Seeing that it was consulted from all eternity between God and Christ, that Christ should be our Redeemer; and seeing God hath actually sent him into the world, and so willingly offers him and all his benefits to us; and Christ so freely offers himself and what he has to be ours: is it not a most equal thing, that we should willingly and heartily receive this offered Savior?

5. And lastly, the most absolute necessity of it. For while we are without faith, we are enemies to God. Without [faith], we can have no access to God, and it's impossible that we should please God. Without faith, we have nothing to do with Christ; we are yet in our sins, under the wrath of God and the curse of the law and eternal condemnation. Without faith, we are shut out from all hope of mercy.

Therefore, earnestly seek faith in all the ways of God's appointment. And cry to God, that he would enlighten your mind that you may know, and open your heart that you may receive Jesus Christ, so freely offered.

Beg of him, that he would give the Spirit of faith, that he would make means successful by his free and sovereign grace.

CHRIST'S PARTICULAR RESPECT TO EVERY BELIEVER IN HIS WORK OF REDEMPTION

(Gal. 2:20, 1728–29)

GALATIANS 2:20 WAS ONE OF EDWARDS' KEYSTONE TEXTS, WHICH HE used to establish and to describe the new life that believers had in Christ, the "principle" they received upon regeneration. He was to explore the meaning of this scripture in "Miscellanies," notebooks, essays, and treatises as a proof-text.[1] He also employed it in this sermon from late 1728 or early 1729, just before or immediately following the death of his grandfather and predecessor Solomon Stoddard (1643–1729). In this case, he discuss the "particularness" of Christ's work of redemption and the "doctrine of particular redemption," all related to the larger issue of divine decrees within predestinarianism.

From the making of the covenant of redemption between the persons of the Trinity in eternity, the Father and the Son knew the identity of every believer. Their names were and still are in the divine mind. Christ, as Redeemer, knew whom he would justify. He had a "dying love" to each believer and came down from heaven knowing each of them. Christ's benefits are distributed equally to all believers.

1. *WJE* 2:168, 491 (*Religious Affections*); *WJE* 7:512 (*The Life of David Brainerd*); *WJE* 8:141 (sermon one, "Charity and Its Fruits"); 8:347 (sermon 13); *WJE* 16:200 (Letter to the Rev. Stephen Williams, in 1746): "I shall not undertake in this letter to go through with the controversy about universal redemption and about the interpretation of those scriptures that speak of Christ's dying for all, etc."; *WJE* 17:281 (sermon); *WJE* 18:534 ("Miscellanies" no. 823, "Perseverance"); *WJE* 19:207 (sermon); *WJE* 19:479 (sermon); *WJE* 27, "*Controversies*" *Notebook*.

Sermons by Jonathan Edwards on the Epistle to the Galatians

In this sermon on Galatians 2:20, Edwards inaugurated his ministry by introducing his parishioners to a concern that would occupy his attention for many years to come—the threat of Arminianism. He particularly takes aim at the Arminian appeal to a general atonement in his treatment of the Apostle's words, "He loved *me* and gave himself for *me*." Edwards argued that these personal pronouns indicate the particular nature of Christ's atoning death. He maintains that, in his death, Christ did not have the face of a blind mass of humanity in mind, but the faces of his people as individuals. The sermon takes on something of a polemical quality as he goes on to offer four points in defense of the definite nature of the atonement or "particularness," in opposition to that of the Arminians, whose advocacy of universal redemption Edwards criticizes as implying that Christ died for those that he knew would not be saved. Other serious consequences follow. "[I]f this doctrine of a particular redemption be denied," Edwards states, "we must not only deny absolute predestination, but God's foreknowledge must also be denied; and if we hold universal redemption, we must say that God does not know what things will come to pass hereafter." Also, Christ's death could potentially have been effective for no one, since, under the Arminian way, choosing grace is dependent on human will. Besides, Scripture affirms that Christ died only for believers.

Believers, therefore, should admire the grace of God to them as particular recipients. Edwards paints a pathetic picture of Christ's sufferings and death to draw forth his listeners' sympathies, concluding with Christ on the cross, where "your name was written on his heart." Saints therefore should consider the "ancientness" and greatness of Christ's love to them, as well as the fact that many are left out of God's book. It is God who makes the difference between the elect and the damned. These considerations, in turn, should strengthen the faith of believers, who can plead the righteousness of Christ, who can know that Christ is mindful of them now, and that Christ will come for their soul when they die. They should devote themselves to Christ, Edwards goes on to counsel, and not abuse the doctrine of election by giving way to fatalism.

This oration proves to be of considerable historical interest for three reasons. First, it provides a very clear articulation of Edwards' view of the extent of the atonement and his placement on the issue within the

Reformed continuum. Likewise, the sermon serves as an example of an early defense of that doctrine in the American Reformed tradition.[2]

Second, Edwards defends limited atonement upon fairly unique exegetical grounds. Galatians 2:20 is not typically used in Reformed commentaries to defend the doctrine of atonement as such. Instead, Reformed commentators typically relied on this text to discuss mortification, vivification, or union with Christ. However, Francis Turretin (1623–87), an important resource for Edwards, proved an exception by using the passage to defend limited against general atonement.[3] Yet Edwards' utilization of this passage exceeds Turretin and many of his Reformed predecessors.

Third, the sermon proves interesting because of Edwards' use of the covenant of redemption to defend his view on the extent of the atonement. The full codification of the covenant of redemption in Reformed theology only gradually developed during the late sixteenth and early seventeenth century. In this sermon, however, we find a clear notion of the topic and an important place for it in the theology of Edwards as he uses the covenant of redemption as the first line of defense against Arminianism.

The sermon illustrates an interpretative discontinuity with past exegetes, as the essence of Edwards' sermon, then, rests on the "particularness" of Christ's work of redemption and the "doctrine of particular redemption." This understanding of the definiteness of atonement is not found in Luther's commentary, which is more concerned with the "true manner of justification set before your eyes, and a perfect example of the assurance of faith."[4] This thought resonates with the words of Perkins: "[I]n these words, the nature and property of justifying faith is set down, which is, to apply the love of God, and the merits of the passion of Christ unto ourselves."[5] In a similar vein are the interpretations of Poole—"*Crucified with Christ*, not only by Justification made partaker of the benefits coming by a Christ crucified but also having Communion"[6]— and Henry—"the apostle concludes this discourse with acquainting us by

---

2. See Brandon J. Crawford, *Jonathan Edwards on the Atonement* (Eugene, OR: Wipf & Stock, 2017).

3. Turretin, *Institutes of Elenctic Theology*, xiv, xiii.

4. Luther, *Commentary upon the Epistle to the Galatians*, 72.

5. Perkins, *A commentarie or exposition, vpon the fiue first chapters of the Epistle to the Galatians*, 133.

6. Poole, *Annotations Upon the Holy Bible*, Vol. II, Galatians II:20.

the doctrine of justification by faith in Christ"[7]—and Locke: "the whole management of myself is conformable to the doctrine of the Gospel, of justification in Christ alone."[8]

In summary, although Edwards refers to the doctrine of justification in the introduction of the sermon, the remainder of the sermon puts an emphasis on the doctrine of particular redemption, and does not follow the consensus of Protestant exegetical commentary since Luther. Perhaps his sidestepping the general course of interpretation reflects his concern about the rise of Arminianism.

Thus, Edwards' sermons on the Galatians need to be read in the historical context whereby pastoral and polemic concern gave way, at times, to the consensus of the Protestant tradition of biblical exegesis.

* * * * *

The manuscript is twelve duodecimo leaves. Edwards' shorthand following the text indicates that he repreached "some" of this sermon a second time with Is. 27:12 as the text. In revising for repreaching, he made some minor revisions.

---

7. Henry, *An Exposition of the Old and New Testament*, VI:516.
8. Locke, *A Paraphrase and Notes on the Epistles of St. Paul to the Galatians*, 44.

Christ's Particular Respect to Every Believer in His Work of Redemption

GALATIANS 2:20

Who loved me, and gave himself for me.

THE APOSTLE IS HERE ANSWERING AN OBJECTION AGAINST JUSTIFICAtion by faith alone, that is, if works have nothing to do in the business of justification, that the gospel would be nothing else but an encouragement to sin, and Christ the minister of sin. Because that men, not expecting to be justified by works, would be careless whether they performed any good works or no.

The Apostle answers, "God forbid. For if I build again the things that I destroyed, I make myself a transgressor" [vv. 17–18]: that there is no force in the objection, because the very nature of justifying faith carries in it the destruction of sin. Truly seeking to be delivered from the grief of sin by Christ, implies in it a hating and forsaking and mortifying of sin; and therefore, they that continue to build what they pretended to destroy, 'tis an evidence that they are yet sinners, and never have truly believed. And although the law be abrogated as to any power of justification of sinners, or condemnation of believers, yet it was not so abrogated as to make way for a licentious life and unrestrained wickedness. Indeed, they that truly believe, are dead to the law; they are convinced by the strictness of the law, that 'tis in vain for 'em to try to be justified by it. They were dead to the law, as to any such end or interest of theirs to be served by, that they might obey the law for a higher and nobler principle than self-love and seeking their own salvation, that is, from a principle of love to God, and a gracious respect unto him. The Apostle says he was crucified with Christ, but yet he lived; he was not dead in sin. Though he was crucified as [to] the law, as to its justifying of him, he was not dead as to a holy life. And this life was by Christ, living in and by the faith of Christ, "who loved me, and gave himself for me"; that is—still pursuing the same argument in answer to their objection—faith in Jesus Christ for justification is so far from encouraging a sinful life, that it is the very true foundation of a holy life: for it gives such a sense of the great love of Jesus Christ in giving himself for us and dying for us, that it makes believers obedient from a principle of gratitude and ingenuity, and not from a spirit of bondage and mere servile fear.

[1.] In these last words, you may, in the first place, observe two things which the Apostle mentions as arguments and motives to him to live to God and Christ, and encouragement to live by faith in Christ:

(1) The love of Christ; and,

(2) The fruit of that love: his giving himself.

[2.] And we observe, in the second place, the particularness of this love of Christ, and of the respect he had to persons that are redeemed by him: he "loved me, and gave himself for me." Not for mankind undistinguishedly, not for the church only, considered in a lump; but he particularly loved me, and had a particular respect to me.

DOCTRINE.

That Christ had a particular respect to every believer in what he did and suffered in the work of redemption.

We shall first explain this; and secondly, vindicate it; and then apply it.

[I.] We shall explain it by the following Propositions:

First Proposition. There was a particular notice taken of every particular believer in the covenant of redemption before the foundation of the world. There was a covenant, an agreement, before the foundation of the world between the Father and the Son concerning the redemption of fallen men. In this covenant, the Son engaged to do all those things that were necessary to sinner's salvation, to come into the world to obey the law, to suffer death; and on the other hand, the Father promised him his mediatorial glory and exaltation, and that he should have a glorious success in his undertaking that, and particularly what success he should have. This was not left uncertain, but the Father engaged how many and who he should save by his great labors and sufferings for men's salvation. Christ knew exactly what would be his success, and what would be his reward.

The eternal Son of God did not undertake this great work without knowing whether it would be to any purpose, or to what purpose it would be. God the Father promised him, that if he would make his soul an offering for sin, he should see that the pleasure of the Lord should prosper in his hands, that he should see the travail of his soul satisfied, and that he should justify many by his knowledge, Is. 53:10–11. And Christ knew how many he should justify. Every particular believer was given to Christ in that eternal covenant of redemption. John 6:37, "All that the Father giveth me shall come to me." Hereby, 'tis evident that the Father has given all believers to Jesus Christ before they come to him. So John 17:2, "Thou hast given him power over all flesh, that he should give eternal life to as many as thou hast given him"; and in the 9th verse, "I pray not for the world, but for them which thou hast given me" out of the world. Every particular believer was given to Christ by the Father before the world was, and Christ looked upon them as his own possession, his reward and his crown. He took delight in them before the earth was created. He looks upon them as his, before they actually believe. John 10:16, "Other sheep have I, which are not of this fold [. . .], and they shall hear my voice." Christ knew from all eternity who are his, and who are not. II Tim. 2:19, "the foundation of God standeth sure, having this seal, The Lord knoweth them that are his." We read of God's foreknowledge of his people. Rom. 8:29, "whom he did foreknow, he also did predestinate."

Christ did as it were write down the names of his people from eternity. He did not only write the names of the countries that should be Christianized, but the names of the persons. Rev. 21:27, "There shall in no wise enter into it anything that defileth, or worketh abomination, or maketh a lie: but they which are written in the Lamb's book of life."

The grace of God and benefits of the gospel were as it were given to believers before the world began; that is, they were given to Christ for them. II Tim. 1:9, "Who hath saved us with an holy calling [. . .], according to his own purpose and grace, which was given us in Christ before the world began."

Second Proposition. He knew everyone of them. When he actually came into the world, and when he laid down his life, he had the names of everyone of them upon his heart.

Everyone was as it were set before his eyes. 'Tis not necessary for us here to inquire how far the human soul of Christ knew as to particulars: there was a very near union between the human soul and the divine nature, and therefore a free communication from the divine knowledge and the human; and therefore, when Christ asked Peter whether he loved him, he replies, "Lord, thou knowest all things," etc. And it is certain that the person of Jesus Christ knew every particular believer when he laid down his life, had them in his actual view. He knew how many sins they had committed or would commit, and what misery their sins deserved. Jesus Christ said when he was upon the earth, John 10:1–14, "I know my sheep." He there speaks of all his sheep which he laid down his life for, as appears by the next verse: not only his disciples that were with him, and those among the Jews that had already believed; but also those among the gentiles, those that were not of that fold, that he says should hereafter hear his voice," as appears by the 16th verse.

Third Proposition. He had a dying love to every particular believer. He had a dying love for every saint that lived before he came into the world, for his people of the Israelitish nation, and those that were before the giving the law and before the flood. And so he had a dying love to all that have been since Christ was upon earth, amongst all Christianized nations, and to all that shall be, to the end of the world. Christ don't only love them after they actually believe in him and love him, but, the Apostle tells us, I John 4:19, "We love him, because he first loved us."

And the shedding of his blood is the fruit of this love. Rev. 1:5, "Who hath loved us, and washed us from our sins in his own blood." But our text[1] is a most direct testimony for this: "Who loved me, and gave himself for me." That is, he had such a love to me, that was great enough to produce such an effect as his giving himself for me. His love to every particular believer is great enough to produce such an effect, as his offering himself a sacrifice to God for him.[2] The love of Christ is not the less to one, because there are a great many that are loved. Christ's love is not divided and distributed amongst his people, a little to one,

---

1. In revising for repreaching, JE deleted "our text" and inserted "Gal. 2:20."
2. In revising for repreaching, JE deleted "His love to every particular believer . . . a sacrifice to God for him" and inserted "great enough to die for me."

and a little to another. 'Tis no hindrance to the entireness and strength of Christ's love to particular persons, that there are such multitudes beloved, any more than it is a hindrance to the perfectness of God's knowledge of a particular thing, that there are so many things that he every moment takes notice of. Men, if they are obliged to take notice of many things at once, can have but an imperfect knowledge of particulars. So if their love is divided amongst many, 'tis the less to particular persons. But 'tis because our knowledge and our love are finite, and may be divided; but the love of Christ is boundless, and because he greatly loves multitudes of others, yet that is no emptying of the fountain of his love, because the fountain is infinite. His dying love is not divided, but is as it were wholly exercised towards every particular believer.

It was Christ's dear love to this and that particular soul that fetched him down from heaven. 'Twas the strength of his love to particular persons, that made him undertake and carried him through so great labors. 'Twas his great love to every particular saint that made him willing to bear shame and spitting, and scourging and crucifying, and the wrath of God.

He had the names of all his people upon his heart when he went through those things, as the high priest was to have the names of the children of Israel on his breastplate, when he was in the exercise of his office; which was appointed on purpose, that it might represent that love and respect that Christ had to particular believers, when he is in the execution of his priestly office, such as working a perfect righteousness, dying and interceding with God in heaven.

Fourth Proposition. And lastly, every particular believer has as much the benefit of what Christ did and suffered, as if it were for him alone. His sins are perfectly satisfied, for all God's wrath ceases, and the whole of the curse of the law is removed; and the believer is brought into a state of favor with God, and has a right to eternal life. Indeed, the degree of blessedness is according to God's will and pleasure; but it is not for want of sufficiency in the blood and righteousness of Christ, that any degree of happiness is not conferred. We can't say that what Christ has done, has made way for such a degree of blessedness, or for such an one. It has made way for any degree of glory that God pleases to bestow, which will be to the filling of the capacity and according to their works.

We are now come, in the

II. Second place, to vindicate this Doctrine. The Arminians hold that Christ died for all alike, without any particular respect to one more than to another; that he died to give all an opportunity of being saved if they would, and no more aimed at the salvation of one than another. Which doctrine we shall prove to be false, by the following arguments:

First. 'Tis absurd to suppose that Christ died for the salvation of those, that he at the same time certainly knew never would be saved. What can be meant by that expression of Christ's dying for the salvation of anyone, but dying with a design that they should be saved by his death? Or dying, hoping that they will be saved, or at least being uncertain but that they will be saved by his death?

When we say that one person does a thing for another, that which is universally understood by such an expression, is that he does it with a design of some benefit to that other person. And 'tis impossible that he should design any benefit to another person, that he certainly knows will have no benefit by it. 'Tis nonsense to say that anything is done with a design that another thing should be done, and to that end that it may be done, at the same time that he has not the least expectation that that other thing ever will be done; and much more, when he perfectly knows it never will.

It matters not in this controversy, whether we suppose an absolute decree or no, if we only allow that God knows all things, that he knows future things before they come to pass, as he declares he does in his Word, and no Christians pretend to deny. But if we don't deny this, it implies a plain contradiction to suppose that Christ died for all in a proper sense.

If it is replied that no other is intended, when they say Christ died for all, than that by his death all have the offer of salvation; so that they may have salvation, if they will accept of salvation, without any expectation or design of Christ that they should be saved by his death: if that be all that is intended, they are against nobody. All that are called Christians own that, by Christ's death, all that live under the gospel have the offer of salvation.

[*Second.*] But if it be said that Christ died for none in no other sense than was seen, that it is impossible {that Christ died for particular persons}, [on] the contrary, this implies, secondly, the same sort of absurdities as the other. As it is evident that Christ did not die for the salvation of all, so it is evident that he must die for some, that is, for these and those particular persons. As it [is] impossible that he should die with a design that they should be saved, that he knew would not be saved by his death;

so 'tis likewise impossible but that he should die for their salvation, with a design to their salvation, that he knew would be saved by his death. For if he died with that design, that some or other should be saved; if it was truly his end, that some sinners should be really saved, and he certainly knew, when he died and before he died, who they would be; if Christ was a free agent in his dying: then it is of necessity that he must die with a design to the salvation of those particular persons. If a man goes into an enemy's country with a design to redeem some captives, and certainly knows beforehand who they will be; if he acts as a free agent, then it necessarily follows that he goes to redeem them particular persons, and no other.

Therefore, if this doctrine of a particular redemption be denied, we must not only deny absolute predestination, but God's foreknowledge must also be denied; and if we hold universal redemption, we must say that God does not know what things will come to pass hereafter, that he is at uncertainties about such things as well as we, and that such things are past finding out with him.

But,

Third. If we suppose that Christ died without any absolute determination that any particular persons should be saved by his death, we must suppose that he undertook to die when he was wholly at uncertainties about the success of his death. If it was, as the Arminians suppose, left only to every man's own determination whether he should have any benefit by Christ's death, without any predetermination of God about it, then God, when he sent Christ into the world to die to save sinners, did not determine whether there should be any success of that great undertaking: for if it was left wholly to man's free will, without anything before that should determine man's will, or make it certain which way man's will should be determined, then it was uncertain, when Christ died, whether one person would be saved by his death; though it might be exceedingly probable, yet it was not absolutely certain. But 'tis unreasonable to suppose that God would leave the success of so great an affair as the death of the Son of God, depending only upon probabilities. 'Tis contrary to that promise, Is. 53:10–11, that when Christ should make his soul an offering for sin, he should see his seed, and should justify many by his knowledge. How could this promise be made, if it was left as a thing undetermined till men's own will determined it, whether there should be one soul converted and justified?

Fourth. The Word of God is plain, that Christ died only for believers. There we are told that Christ died for the church. Eph. 5:25, "Christ loved the church, and gave himself for it." Christ tells us that he dies for his sheep. John 10:14–15, "I know my sheep [. . .] and I lay down my life for the sheep." Christ don't not so much as pray for them that ben't of the elect; much less doth he die for them. John 17:9, "I pray not for the world, but for those which thou hast given me out of the world."

APPLICATION

Use I. If it be thus, that Christ had a particular respect to every believer in what he did and suffered in the work of redemption, what great reason have believers to admire the grace of God towards them. It is much more for 'em to [be] the objects of such a particular love, than if they were only common partakers of a general kindness to mankind. As a prince may love his country, and may very much lay out himself for the peace and prosperity of it, and all or most of his subjects may partake of the happy influence of his reign. It is not only thus, but Christ perfectly knew everyone of those that were his; he knew them all by name. Ex. 33:12, "I know thee by name." God the Father, when he sent the Son into the world, he knew all whom he loved and sent his Son to redeem; and the Lord Jesus Christ, when he came into the world, and when he came to the cross, he knew them and loved them that he was about to die for.

If you have believed in Christ, he knew you before he came into the world, and was better acquainted with you than your nearest friends are now. And when he was upon earth, when he hung upon the cross, your name was written upon his heart; you was set as a seal upon his heart; your name was engraven there in indelible characters. He was in the form of God, and thought it no robbery to be equal with God; and it was because he loved you, that he humbled himself and took on him the form of a servant, and appeared in the likeness of men. 'Twas because he loved you, that he lived three or four and thirty years in the world in a low condition, and underwent so much hardships, and went through such labors. 'Twas for you that he sweat such drops of blood in the garden; when he stood amongst the soldiers with his crown of thorns upon his head, his heart overflowed with love to you. And 'twas from love to you that his blood run out of his veins and from his heart, and his soul was in such darkness and amazement. His love to you was stronger than death; his pains and his agonies were exceedingly great, but his love was greater. The foresight of the great benefit that would accrue to you by these sufferings, made him willingly go through.

That was Christ's motive to come into the world; his delights were with the sons of men, and that was his encouragement. That was the promise of the Father in the covenant of redemption that encouraged him to undertake such sufferings, that if he would make his soul an offering for sin, he should see his seed. 'Twas his joyful expectation of saving of you, and other particular persons which the Father had given him, that made him cheerfully to come and undertake his exceedingly great work.

I shall mention several things that are particularly worthy of your consideration, to excite your admiration of this love of Christ:

First. The ancientness of it. It was not only in the heart of Jesus Christ when he became incarnate and when he was upon the cross, but long before. Your name was not first written upon his heart about that time, but it had been there of old. It was there when God gave the law from Mount Sinai. God, in that transaction, had not only a respect to the children of Israel, but to his elect to the end of the world, a respect to you personally in it. And it was there when the flood of waters was upon the earth; in the midst of that dreadful dispensation, Christ remembered his love to you and to his other elect that were not yet born, and appointed an ark for the saving of Noah and his family. And it was not only them personally that God manifested his love to at that time, but all their elect posterity that were virtually in the ark at that time, and were as it were saved from a state of nonexistence in it.

Christ had your name upon his heart when he created the world. He remembered his love to you when he created this lower world. This world was made principally for the elect, that it might be a place wherein they might be prepared for eternal blessedness. Christ tells us, Prov. 8:31, that when God laid the foundations of the earth, then his "delights were with the sons of men." And Christ remembered his love to you, when he made heaven to be a place of blessedness. He made it beautiful and glorious, and prepared it to be a place of delight and happiness for you to dwell in. See Matt. 20:23, "to sit on my right hand and on my left [. . .] shall be given to them for whom it is prepared of my Father." So Matt. 25:34, "Come [. . .], inherit the kingdom prepared for you from the foundation of the world."

And the love of Christ to you was no new thing then: it was a thing of old standing, when the foundation of the heavens and the earth were laid. Christ had a book written, the Lamb's book of life, wherein your name had been written from all eternity. God the Father and the Son did as it were consult together from the days of eternity about the redemption of lost men, and made a covenant together, and then was your name mentioned as one of those that should be redeemed.

How wonderful is this, that God should have such a respect to a little worm of the dust, a sinful, defiled worm. How wonderful that Christ should set his love upon such an one. Job 7:17, "What is man, that thou shouldest magnify him? and that thou shouldest set thine heart upon him?" And Ps. 144:3, "Lord, what is man, that thou takest knowledge of him! or the son of man, that thou makest account of him!"

Second. Consider how many others there are whose names were left out, that Christ had no respect to in the work of redemption. When Christ came into the world, and when he died, there are vast multitudes that he had no love to: he knew them not; they were utter strangers to him; their names were not written upon his heart; they never were in the Lamb's book of life. When the covenant of redemption was made, there was no mention made of them. They were always left out of God's gracious respect in all the great works that God has wrought. They never were given to Jesus Christ, nor were they ever owned by him, nor never will be owned.

But God has chosen you according to his good pleasure, and has set his love upon you; was pleased to think thoughts of pity and love towards you before the world began. You are not naturally one whit better than others; you are born as filthy as they, and have provoked God as much as they, at least as much as many of them: and yet what a vast difference has God put between you and them, that Christ should single you out to lay down his life for you, and to choose you and call you out of the world to see his marvelous light.

Third. Consider the greatness of this love. We can describe the degree of love no otherwise than by the effects of it: and dying is the greatest effect. 'Tis the highest argument of the truth of love, that the lover is willing to suffer without any reward; and it is an argument of the truth, and also of the great strength of it, when the lover is willing to suffer even to death for the beloved. With such a love has Christ loved you, and with such a love has he loved you from eternity.

Christ's Particular Respect to Every Believer in his Work of Redemption

The greatness of this love also appears by the greatness of those enjoyments, which are bestowed upon believers as the fruits of it. There is the pardon of sin and peace with God, [which] is an infinite benefit, because 'tis a freedom from the eternal wrath of God, which is an infinite evil. There is sanctification, the Spirit of God, which is given. There is the merciful and watchful care of providence in this world. And there is eternal glory, a crown of life which is promised them; and there is the resurrection and glorification of the body, and so the eternal glory of the whole man with Christ.

Seeing, therefore, the love of Christ has been so wonderful to you, see that you admire it and praise and glorify God for it. Don't forget what great and wonderful things God has done for you.

Use II is to strengthen the faith of believers. If Christ had a particular respect to every believer in what he did and suffered, then they may undoubtedly safely trust in Jesus Christ. The Apostle made this improvement of it, as is implied in the verse of our text:[3] "the life which I now live in the flesh," says the Apostle, "I live by the faith of the Son of God, who loved me, and gave himself for me."

First. If it be thus, doubtless we[4] may confidently plead before God the righteousness and satisfaction of Jesus Christ, seeing 'tis that which was wrought out for 'em from a particular respect to them, and from a particular dying love to them. Jesus Christ wrought out this righteousness on purpose, that you might be justified by it. Therefore, doubtless 'tis safe appearing in it before God. If you trust in God, [he] will undoubtedly justify you upon the account of it.

Second. If it be so, they may be assured that [Christ] is not unmindful of them now. If he was mindful of them when he laid down his life; if he was mindful of them before the foundation of the world; if he had their names upon his heart from all eternity: then surely he won't forget them, when they actually are come into being. You may be sure that Christ is mindful of you at the right hand of God; seeing he has shed his blood for you, he won't forget to plead that [which] he has done and suffered for you, before the Father. Christ prayed for you above seventeen hundred years ago. John 17:20, "I don't pray for these alone, but for them also

---

3. In revising for repreaching, JE deleted "the verse of our text" and inserted "Gal. 2:20."

4. In revising for repreaching, JE deleted "we" and inserted "this is a strengthening upon faith accounts."

which shall believe on me through their word." And surely Christ won't forget to pray for you, now you are actually come into the world, and have believed on his name.

You may be sure that he is mindful of you; he is mindful of your soul. You may with great confidence leave your soul in his hands, and trust in him to strengthen you against your corruptions, to preserve you from falling, and to fit you for his eternal glory. He is not unmindful of your outward man; you may safely cast your care upon him, for he careth for you. Can you think that [Christ, who] died for you, will forget you? A woman may sooner forget her sucking child, than Christ forget you, who has travailed in pain with you. No, his eye is ever upon you, by day and by night. You may trust in him in all your afflictions and troubles which you meet with, all the difficulties and distresses you are called to go through. Christ won't forget his covenant that he has sealed with his blood. You have not a high priest that cannot be touched with a feeling of your infirmities: he has felt more pain and affliction than ever you did, and he felt it for you. It is a blessed thing in affliction, to have such a merciful high priest to trust in.

Third. If it be so, you may be assured that Christ will take care of your soul when you come to die. If he should not do that, he would lose his end in dying for you. He died that your soul might be saved, and made blessed forever. And surely Christ will take care that he don't miss of his end in enduring such great sufferings. You was given to Jesus Christ by the Father before the world was; and all those that the Father gave him, he looks upon as his jewels, and he won't fail to wake up his jewels. He will have them that were given him, along with him where he is. John 17:24, "Father, I will that those whom thou hast given me, be with me where I am, that there they may be also; that they may behold my glory, which thou hast given me: for thou lovedst me before the foundation of the world."

Therefore, you may with great safety put your trust in Christ, whether in life or in death. When you are passing through the valley of the shadow of death, you need fear none ill, for you may be assured that Christ is with you.

Use III is to *Exhort* you wholly to devote yourself[5] to Jesus Christ, and live to him. You have heard that Christ has loved you and given

---

5. In revising for repreaching, JE deleted "you" and inserted "believers" and deleted "yourself" and inserted "themselves."

himself for you: and don't he deserve that you should so love him, as to give yourself to him? This is but a little thing to what that was; 'tis a small recompense of his labors and pains, which he underwent.

Therefore, make that improvement of it, which the Apostle did. Crucify the flesh and live to God; devote yourself wholly to Jesus Christ, and let his glory be the end of your lives. Study how you may live more to his honor, and bring forth more fruit to his praise, and adorn his doctrine in all things. If you don't, you will be exceeding ungrateful. If you were but sufficiently sensible of the greatness and undeservedness of the love of Christ, you would be exceedingly set to live to his glory.

Use IV is of *Caution,* to caution natural persons from abusing this Doctrine to discourage them in using means for their salvation. Natural men, through the devil's temptation, are often apt to discourage themselves by the doctrines of absolute election and Christ's particular redemption; are ready to think, if the case be so, 'tis in vain to use any means for their salvation. But this is very unreasonable; there is no sort of reason for any such discouragement from it. If there be any grounds, it must be in one of these two ways: either that you see some sort of sign that you are not one of the elect, and one that Christ died for; or else that the means that you use for your salvation, will be the less probable to be effectual for it. If there be any good reason at all of discouragement, it must be one of these. But you han't, for:

First. If you are but willing to use the means for your salvation, you see no sign in the world that Christ did not die for you. If you imagine you do, it is the devil that deceives you, to make you think neither that devil nor you can see any sort of sign that you are not elected by God. God has kept it in his own breast; the book is sealed with seven seals, and there is none in heaven nor the earth, nor under the earth, that are able to open that book, but only the Lamb. The worst sign is being careless and regardless of your soul-concerns, being given up to a careless, senseless, regardless[6] spirit, a being given up to ways of vice and immorality; such as are so, it looks more darkly upon. But if you are but willing to use the means, you can see no sign of your being reprobated.

Second. The means you use, ben't at all the less probable to be effectual, for there being only a chosen number that Christ died for. If God had not elected none, nor made no decree about it, yet the success of means

---

6. In revising for repreaching, JE deleted "careless" and "regardless" and inserted "stupid."

would depend upon his efficacy: they would be effectual only where he made them so. It would be in that respect then, as it is now.

Yea, 'tis more probable that means that are diligently and duly used will be successful. For those that God has elected, he has decreed should be converted in this way: he has joined the due use of means and the end very much together in his decree. When God therefore stirs up diligently and steadfastly to use means, it looks probable, as if God had an intention of mercy. Whereas if God had not decreed those to be the means for the obtaining of this end, one could give no sort of guess about the end by the means. Those that earnestly used means, would be no more likely to obtain [mercy], than those that used none at all.

THE GOSPEL NO ENCOURAGEMENT TO SIN
(Gal. 2:17, 1731–32)

LIKELY PREACHED TOWARDS THE END OF 1732, EDWARDS MUSTERED ALL of his rational and theological faculties to curb any pretense that justification by faith alone encouraged sin. In his exposition, Edwards begins by considering the motivations by which sinners manipulate the teaching of the gospel to sanction ungodly behavior. Instead, he argued, if rightly understood, the gospel "will not have any tendency to promote wickedness of life, or to encourage any person to go on in sin, or to allow of any one sinful act." He then proceeded to support his doctrine with twelve arguments.

What Edwards is concerned about here, as was the Apostle in Galatians, was that those who professed themselves to be justified in Christ nonetheless continued in sin. As such, many make the gospel a "foundation for sin," because of what they read about the infiniteness of God's mercy, Christ's satisfaction for the sins of all, the worthlessness of individual righteousness for justification, and the pardon offered on "hearty acceptance" of Christ. Yet, the gospel is no encouragement to sin, for it states that sin is forbidden, that the duties of the law must be followed, that God's wrath against sin abides, that universal obedience is still necessary, that it provides no encouragement to commit even one more sin, that there is no assurance of the continuance of life, that great sinners are more exposed to damnation than others, that the ungodly are exposed to great punishment, and dreadful punishment is threatened to those who go on in sin. All of this promotes obedience to Christ, insofar as the gospel teaches that the obedience of fallen creatures, as far as it goes, is acceptable; that eternal life is attainable by such obedience as sinners are capable of; and that no one act of sincere obedience will miss of its eternal reward. The gospel therefore affords "powerful motives" to avoid sin and obey God's commands.

In this defense, some of Edwards' challenges are worth mentioning. Edwards reminded his audience that, although the justified are freed from the law as a covenant, it is still a "rule of life." He reinforces for them God's immutable character and exhorts them to consider how the gospel reveals God's hatred of sin and his wrath against it. He sounds an unusual note when he informs his audience that though they are not justified by works, "universal obedience is as truly necessary to salvation under the gospel as it was under the first commandment," or first covenant. By that he appears to mean that obedience is a necessary by-product of justifying faith. One can only speculate as to what he intended by "universal" obedience, but he appears to mean either obedience in all believers or an obedience that extends to all of life.

Of further interest is Edwards' use of the scholastic distinction between the sufficiency and efficiency of Christ's atonement. He frequently appeals to these scholastic categories but decries pleading the sufficiency of Christ's work as an excuse for sin, writing starkly: "God don't bring to Christ everyone that the blood of Christ is sufficient for." His final exhortation is similarly striking, as he threatens (using Matt. 11:21 as a prooftext) that "they that go to hell now, that have lived under the gospel, will go to a great deal worse hell, than if there had been no gospel."

At one point, Edwards gives the audience a glimpse of his understanding how the saints reflect on hell. In the tenth defense of his doctrine, he considers how the godly respond to thoughts of hell. Although they are secure from damnation, nevertheless, thoughts of hell are sometimes useful in motivating the saints' greater fidelity to God. He writes, "When persons are strong in grace or have grace in a lively exercise, they don't need fear of hell to restrain 'em from sin"; nevertheless, "sometimes, when grace is weak or lies asleep, and the saints are in an ill frame, they commonly need the fear of hell to restrain and curb their lusts, and make them strictly to avoid sin."

For Application, Edwards begins by instructing his listeners in the wisdom of God's work of redemption, wherein God gives mercy and provides a Savior. The wicked who taken encouragement to sin from the gospel are unreasonable. Indeed, what does give encouragement to sin? If not the gospel, neither is it law, nor reason or the light of nature; all conspire to teach obedience. Instead, he argues that reason teaches that God exists and that he is a rightful king who demands obedience and punishes disobedience. He maintains that even pagans believe this. Hence, the evidence of reason provides an apology for the truth of Scripture's teaching on future punishment and on the need to flee to Christ for refuge. The final Use rehearses the points in the first and second heads of the doctrine, showing the encouragements that sinners take from the gospel to sin, and then reasserting that such encouragements have no basis.

What precipitated this discourse? Perhaps two challenges of Edwards' young ministry contributed to its composition. Following his elevation to sole pastor of the Northampton church in 1729, Edwards sensed an urgent need to stem the tide of Arminianism. This precipitated a number of printed and unpublished discourses, including this one, on the nature of justification. Reformed theology's Arminian critics have often charged the doctrine of justification by faith with producing presumption, antinomianism, and licentiousness. There can be little doubt that Edwards had his Arminian critics in mind when he preached this sermon in 1732.

He also likely considered the youth of his congregation. Early in his ministry, adolescents in the town of Northampton indulged in behavior that troubled Edwards, particularly in the area of sexuality. It is likely that Edwards felt that these youths appeased their consciences by manipulating the teaching of justification and using it as a license for sin. When he preached his four-part series on justification by faith in 1734, the series caused a great deal of religious concern in the town, even amongst some of these licentious youths. In either case, Edwards' sermon would have provided a challenge to the objections of Arminians and the godless lifestyle of the young people of Northampton. Herein, this sermon illustrates Edwards' focus throughout his ministry on the religious behavior and speech of youth.

Further, this sermon nicely illustrates the relationship between Edwards' exegetical, theological, and pastoral work, as contemporaneously written entries on the nature of justification in his "Blank Bible" and "Miscellanies," as well as this sermon, interact. In the "Blank Bible" entry on Galatians 2:18, part of the text of this sermon, Edwards dwells on hatred of sin as part or evidence of justification; and in "Miscellanies" no. 504, on "Condition of Justification. Repentance. Faith," he states that for God's offer of freedom believers must will in their hearts to "quit" sin, concluding, "by faith we destroy sin."[1]

* * * * *

The manuscript is twenty-seven duodecimo-sized leaves, comprising three preaching units, with the second beginning at the fifth subhead of the second head of the Doctrine, and the third at the Application.

---

1. *WJE* 18:102; *WJE* 23:183, and *WJE* 24:1080.

The Gospel No Encouragement to Sin

GALATIANS 2:17-18

But if, while we seek to be justified by Christ, we ourselves also are found sinners, is therefore Christ the minister of sin? God forbid. For if I build again the things which I destroyed, I make myself a transgressor.

THESE WORDS, AND THE DISCOURSE OF WHICH IT IS A PART, ARE INTROduced by the Apostle's giving an account how he withstood Peter at Antioch in conforming to the legal and self-righteous Jews.

There were many of the Jews who, after they turned Christians, yet continued very zealous of the law of Moses, and especially was it so with the Jewish Christians at Jerusalem. They were, notwithstanding their profession of Christ as the Messiah, yet fond of circumcision and other ceremonies of the law of Moses and the customs which they had been bred up in, one of which was to avoid eating with the gentiles.

Peter knew better, for he was the first of the apostles that had it revealed to him that it was lawful freely to converse with gentiles as with Jews, by the vision that he had when he was sent to Cornelius [Acts 10]. And when he was at Antioch he used the liberty; he freely conversed with the gentiles and ate with them. But when afterwards some came from James, that is, from the church at Jerusalem, which was especially under the oversight of the apostle James, he withdrew and separated himself, and avoided the company of the gentiles, lest he should offend those Jews: and hereby he was guilty of an unwarrantable compliance with their legal and self-righteous practices.

Upon which, the apostle Paul, who was there and observed him, reproved him, as he gives an account in the 14th verse: "But when I saw that they walked not uprightly according to the truth of the gospel, I said unto Peter before them all, If thou, being a Jew, livest after the manner of gentiles, and not as do the Jews, why compellest thou the gentiles to live as do the Jews?" The giving an account of this leads the Apostle to observe of [how] little avail works are in the affair of justification, contrary to the notion that those legal Jews were ready to entertain: "We who are Jews by nature, and not sinners of the gentiles, knowing that a man is not justified by the works of the law, but by the faith of Jesus Christ."

But here in the text is an objection proposed and answered, against this doctrine of being justified by faith alone without works, viz., that this makes Christ the minister of sin, and the gospel an encouragement to sin. For if we are justified by Christ from the guilt of all sin, and good works are of no use in the affair of justification, then what are works good for? What matter is it how many sins we commit, as long as we may be justified by Christ from all of them, let them be as many as they will? And what matter how few good works we do, as long as they do nothing towards our justification? And so, is not Christ, while he is a justifier of ungodly men, an encourager of ungodliness? The Apostle by no means allows what is objected, and answers, "If I build again the things which I destroyed, I make myself a transgressor."

That is faith in Jesus Christ, by which we come to be justified by him, and on his account is of such a nature, that it implies the destruction of sin that accompanies it, yea, is included in it—the divorcing of the heart from sin, a renunciation of it.

And therefore, if we build again this which we seemingly destroyed, we make ourselves transgressors. We prove ourselves yet to be in sin, and show that we have never truly believed in Christ and sought to be justified by him.

DOCTRINE

The gospel is no encouragement to sin

That is, the revelation the gospel makes of the mercy of God and redemption of Christ, if rightly understood, no way tends so to encourage and forward a future sinning.

The Gospel No Encouragement to Sin

The gospel does afford encouragement for sinners, but it don't encourage them in sin. There is a difference between affording encouragement for sinners, and encouraging them in sin. The gospel affords encouragement for sinners: that is, here is encouragement for them to forsake their sins and turn to God, that may do so greatly to their own advantage. But there can reasonably, and with a right understanding, be no encouragement fetched from the gospel to go on sinning, or for the commission of any future sin so as to promote the commission of it, instead of opposing and hindering it. It is true that the revelation is very often abused to this last purpose, but very unreasonably. And 'tis a perverting of the gospel to a purpose that is quite contrary to its nature.

Here I would, first, take notice of some things in the gospel whence men are often wont perversely to encourage themselves in sin; second, show that the revelation which the gospel makes is no encouragement to sin.

I. I would take notice of some things in the gospel, which sinners often mistake to have foundation of encourage[ment] for 'em to go on in sin.

First. The gospel reveals the infiniteness of the mercy of God. The goodness of God was manifested in the creation, then appeared in the covenant of works, but not his mercy. The mercy of God, which is his goodness to the sinful and miserable, was unknown before the gospel revealed it. But now the gospel has revealed this glorious perfection of the Divine Being, and opened that infinite fountain. Whoever imagined before that God had any mercy to the sinful, to rebels against himself, and those that were his enemies? But the gospel reveals that God has mercy, and not only so, but that there are no bounds to his mercy; that there is mercy sufficient for the greatest sinner.

The gospel reveals that there is mercy enough in God for sinners, if they do go on in sin. If they commit never so many sins more than they have done, yet the mercy of God will be sufficient.

Many take encouragement from hence to go on in sin.

Second. The gospel reveals that Christ hath suffered enough to satisfy for the sins of all mankind. Not only that God hath in himself mercy sufficient for the sinful, and for the most sinful, but that that mercy has exercised itself by actually providing a Savior for sinners; and declares that Christ, the eternal Son of God, has actually died and shed his blood, which is sufficient to cleanse from all sin.

Third. The gospel reveals that there is no need of our righteousness for our justification, and that it avails nothing in that affair. It teaches that if we do live never so well, never so strictly according to God's commands, we shall not upon the account of that at all be accepted into God's favor, and as being of eternal life; that if we are never so exact in our obedience, God will not be at all the less angry with us for the sins we have committed upon that account.

It reveals to us that there is no need of our obedience in order to justification, or that we may be justified by it. It remains that we must be justified and accepted of God through the obedience and righteousness of another, {and} that that obedience, by which we are to be justified, is already performed.

Fourth. The gospel offers pardon and salvation to every creature only for a hearty acceptance. It reveals not only that there is an attribute of mercy in God sufficient for sinners, and that God has been pleased to exercise that mercy, so far as to provide a Savior that has actually made satisfaction and wrought out righteousness, that is sufficient to justify the greatest sinner. But more than that, justification is actually offered to everyone that will heartily accept of it as offered, without any more difficult terms, let him be he who will, and though he be one that has gone on in sin against light.

Now upon these accounts, sinners often look upon the gospel as encouragement to sin. They take encouragement from it to allow themselves in the commission of sin. They think with themselves that if the mercy of God be infinite, that he is a being that is full of compassion and gracious, so that he has no pleasure in the death of a sinner, and don't afflict willingly nor grieve the children of men; God won't have the heart to cast them into hell, and torment 'em there to all eternity. They flatter themselves that God, being so merciful, if they cry to him for mercy a great while hence, he will have mercy upon them. If they beg mercy on him, and make piteous moan on their deathbed, they think they shall not be refused. They think if God's mercy be all-sufficient, then it will be sufficient for their pardon and acceptance; it will be sufficient for them, though they go on in sin yet a great while longer. If Christ's sufferings be sufficient to satisfy for the sins of all the world, then they will be sufficient to satisfy for their sins, though they go on in sin yet for many years.

The Gospel No Encouragement to Sin

If they ben't justified by their own righteousness and obedience, but by the obedience of another, then what need is there of their obeying? Why mayn't they neglect obedience and go on in sin, seeing that the law has been obeyed for 'em already?

And again, if pardon and salvation be offered to everyone whatsoever only for accepting of it, then they think with themselves, why won't it do for them to go on in sin still and accept of mercy many years hence? Salvation will be offered to 'em then as well as now, and upon the same terms. If they may have pardon at any time only for accepting it, what haste need they be in about it?

So again, some that look upon themselves as converted, think that seeing the promises of salvation is absolute to them that have once experienced a work of conversion. They but fall away from a state of salvation, do hence encourage themselves in their sins; they are bold to indulge their lusts and gratify their carnal and unlawful inclinations. For they think that, seeing they are converted, now there is no danger, they may give themselves a swing; now they can't fall from grace. Heaven is sure to 'em, let 'em live as wickedly as they will.

Fifth. The gospel does absolutely promise salvation to them that have once believed in Christ. So that those that are converted, they are certainly to obtain eternal life. So sure as a man can be that he is converted, so sure may he be that he shall be saved. Though he may afterwards fall into sin, yet 'tis impossible they should miss of salvation.

But,

II. Notwithstanding, the gospel is not an encouragement unto sin. If the gospel revelation be right taken up, as it is in itself, as it relates to us, it will not have any tendency to promote wickedness of life, or to encourage any person to go on in sin, or to allow of any one sinful act. Which will appear by considering the following things:

First. Every sin is as much forbidden of God now under the gospel as ever it was. God doth as strictly forbid us that live under the gospel, the commission of any one, even the least, sin, the least deviation from his law in any point whatsoever—in thought, word or deed—as he did our first parents under the first covenant.

We have, in no instance whatsoever, any allowance to commit sin, in any the least particular—in thought, word or deed—than our first parents while in innocency. God doth as strictly require us to obey all his commands, and in every particular, and at all times, as ever he did Adam and Eve.

We are required to obey the same moral law, and as strictly required to be subject in every particular to God's positive precepts that he gives us now, as Adam and Eve were to abstain from eating the forbidden fruit; and we are required by the same authority. It would be a contradiction to suppose that God allows any, in the least instance at any time, to disobey his command: for if he allows it, then it ceases to be his command; for he can't allow a thing, and yet it be contrary to his command at the same time. If he allows, he don't forbid.

The law of God remains still in full force as a declaration of the will of the Lawgiver. Every part that it consists of, God doth as much command and require as ever. It is now as much a rule for us to walk by as ever. The law is what we are free from as a covenant, but not as a rule of life.

Though the gospel reveals the infinite mercy and grace of God to sinners, yet the mercy that is revealed don't consist at all in giving of us more liberty or allowance now than then. It don't consist in dispensing with some of his precepts that before were obligatory, or in giving us any greater latitude. Our obligation is the same now as then.

Christ hath suffered indeed enough to satisfy for all sins, let them be never so great and many; but he did not thereby purchase a license for us to go on in sin, or to commit any one sin. The gospel reveals that there is no need of our obedience, that we may be justified upon the account of it. But it don't reveal to us that we are not obliged to it.

Second. The gospel does more fully bring to light the duties of the law. The law, as a rule of life, is not only not abolished by the gospel, but 'tis abundantly illustrated; the commands and duties of it are set in a most clear light.

The precepts and duties of the moral law are nowhere so clearly and fully revealed, as they were revealed by Christ and his apostles. The gospel brings to light many duties of the moral law, which, if we were left to the light of nature, we should be greatly in the dark about by reason of the obscurity of the light of nature through the corruption of nature.

We have nowhere such a perfect and a full exhibition of the precepts and duties of the moral law, as we have in the rules of the gospel. The gospel discovers the strictness and spirituality of the law, how that God forbids sins of thought and inclination, as well as of outward behavior, Matt. 5. The duties of the law of God are abundantly more fully revealed by Christ and the evangelical dispensation, than it was by Moses and the prophets under the legal dispensation.

By this, it appears that God is not more careless of his law, and how men break it now, than formerly, inasmuch as he is careful to make such a full and particular revelation of {it}, and to insist so mu[ch upon it].[1]

Third. The gospel does more fully reveal the terribleness of his wrath against [sin]. God don't hate sin less now than he did before the fall. His hatred of sin arises from the immutable holiness of his nature; and unless the nature of God should change, his hatred of sin and his displeasure against it must always remain the same.

So God still reveals his hatred of sin by the forbidding of it, and his wrath against it by the punishing of it. Yea, God never gave such testimonies of it, as those which the gospel sets before us.

It never appeared any other way how irreconcilably God and sin are at enmity, how greatly God is provoked by it and how terrible his wrath is against it, and how inexorable his justice in punishing of it, as by the sufferings of Christ which the gospel tells us of.

This gives a more full discovery of these things than that eternal death, which the law threatened. It was a greater discovery of it, than if every sin that men commit were punished with this eternal damnation.

'Tis true that the gospel makes a revelation of the infinite mercy of God, but not only so, but it at the same time discovers the justice of God. It discovers the inflexibleness of justice, and that he will by no means show mercy to the prejudice of justice, Ex. 34:7.

There is a greater discovery of God's grace in this gospel than ever there was before, and not only so, but there is also a greater discovery of the vindictive justice of God than ever there was before. So that the revelation of the mercy of God that the gospel makes, don't render him at all the less the object of fear and dread (though it represents him as more the object of love and trust), because that it makes a more full discovery of his justice at the same time.

God's inflicting the full punishment of sin on his Son, when he had taken the guilt of it upon him, is a greater manifestation of the strictness

---

1. MS damage.

and inflexibility of the justice of God, than the damnation of ungodly men would have been.

Because the sufferings of Christ, though but temporary, were fully equivalent to the eternal sufferings of all mankind. And then, the justice of God has more of a trial when guilt lies upon his own dear Son, than when it lies upon mere men, because his Son is a person infinitely near and dear to God; and if God will inflict the whole of the punishment of sin when he takes the guilt of it upon him, it is a more clear evidence that his hatred of sin is infinite and his justice inflexible, in revenging it inflexible, than his punishing worms of the dust that are mere creatures and don't stand in so near a relation to God.

If God revealed mercy for the pardon of sin and for the justification of the sinner without the satisfaction of justice, without any reparation made for the wrong done to the divine majesty, it would be an encouragement to sin. The authority of God would thereby become contemptible and his law not esteemed sacred. But now, there is no room for any such thing, when it appears by the sufferings of Christ that God would by no means clear the guilty, and that it was so dreadful a thing to disobey and offend God, that nothing less than the blood of a divine person could expiate such a crime. This has a tendency to possess the minds of all with an awful sense of the sacredness of the commands of God, and so to make men have a dreadful thought of sin.

Fourth. Though according [to] the tenor of the gospel, obedience be not that by which we are justified, yet universal obedience is as truly necessary to salvation under the gospel, as it was under the first covenant. Perfect obedience is not necessary now to salvation, but universal obedience, though it be not the thing that brings to an interest in Christ, and upon the account of which they are looked upon as having a title to his satisfaction and righteousness, yet 'tis what is a necessary attendant and effect of that which is the proper condition of a title to Christ's righteousness.

Faith is the proper condition of justification, but obedience, an universal obedience, is what is necessary to salvation, because 'tis a natural, necessary fruit of it. If true faith is necessary to salvation, then the things which are true and proper evidences of the nature of that faith are also necessary. Because true faith always carries the evidences or proper marks of itself with [it], if there be a faith that is without the proper signs of true faith, that is an evidence that it is not true. Faith in Jesus Christ is the gate through which persons enter into life. But a way of universal obedience is the narrow way, Matt. 7:14. Now the walking in the way is as truly necessary in order to salvation, as the entering the gate.

So that although the mercy of God is sufficient to save the greatest sinner, and Christ has satisfied for all sins, and none are justified on the account of their obedience, yet there can be no encouragement fetched from all this for any to allow themselves in any sin: for though men ben't justified by obedience, yet the nature of that faith by which men are justified, is such that men can't have it, and at the same time live in the stated allowance of any sin. It is a thing of a nature contrary to an allowed sinning, and incompatible with it.

A sinful and wicked life, though the wickedness of life consists only in the gratification of some one lust, exposes to damnation as well under the gospel as under the first covenant, and does as certainly prove a man to be in a state of damnation and exposed to the wrath and curse of God as it did then. The very condition of justification implies a destruction of sin, in its principle and acts too.

An universal obedience only being necessary to escape damnation and to the obtaining eternal life, tends to promote obedience more than if perfect obedience were necessary. For in that universal obedience is necessary, it is necessary that men should sincerely endeavor and aim at obeying the whole law of God, to neglect no command at no time, and to allow of sin in no case; to obey as far as is possible. Now if perfect obedience were necessary, and it were absolutely required in order to salvation, it could not promote obedience any further than that men should endeavor to obey in all things; it could not promote obedience no further than to make men's obedience universal; it would not be perfect, for that is impossible in the present corrupt state of man's nature.

It could not possibly, therefore, promote obedience any further than the requiring of universal obedience. And it would not promote it so far: for if perfect obedience were necessary, men would soon find it was impossible and would cease to endeavor it, and when they see that they had failed of what was absolutely necessary to life, they would give themselves the reins and would no longer endeavor to fulfill the impossible condition of eternal life.

But now an universal obedience is possible for men in this corrupt state. It is a thing attainable, and therefore there is encouragement for men earnestly to seek it.

So that if any take encouragement from the revelation which the gospel makes to neglect an universal obedience, it must be from a misunderstanding of things.

If there be any that think themselves converted, and so take encouragement from the absolute promise of eternal life to them that are converted, statedly to allow themselves in a way of sin, it arises from a misunderstanding of the things of the gospel, as particularly from a misunderstanding of the nature of that faith and conversion which the gospel requires as necessary to salvation. And if there be any that are seeking to get into a state of salvation, if they are hoping to it in any other way than a way of earnestly endeavoring in all things to obey God's commandments, this arises from a gross mistake and misunderstanding of things. They are seeking for that which, in the way they are in, they are never like to obtain.

The gospel is so far from being an encouragement to sin, that whoever truly receives and embraces it, must and will live a holy life. Heb. 12:14, "Without holiness, no man shall see [the Lord]." I John 2:3–4, "hereby we do know that we know him, if we keep his commandments. He that saith, I know him, and keepeth not his commandments, is a liar, and the truth is not in him."[2]

Fifth.[3] The gospel gives no just encouragement to ungodly men to go on to commit one more sin: for if they do so, God has not in the gospel promised that ever will he give 'em repentance of it. The gospel does indeed reveal that whatever sins men commit, upon their repentance they shall be pardoned. But this repentance is not a thing in their own power. Repentance is no more in their power than pardon is, and though the gospel promises pardon upon repentance, yet the gospel nowhere promises repentance to him that is yet going on in sin.

The ungodly man, when his lusts stir up to commit another sin, he has this to consider: "If I commit this sin which I am now tempted to, I don't know whether ever God will give me repentance of it as long as I live. I don't know but that God may be provoked by it forever to leave me in sin."

The gospel tells us of God's pardoning great sinners upon repentance. And it also gives us information of such a thing as God's punishing

---

2. End of first preaching unit. JE repeats the text, which is here omitted.
3. MS: "6." JE misnumbered this and the subsequent subpoints in this head.

sin with sin; his giving men up to sin; his judicially leaving men to an impenitent heart, and an evil heart of unbelief in departing from the living God; [his giving them over to a] reprobate mind, Rom. 1:24, 26–28; to their own hearts' lusts; of his being provoked to give 'em over to such a hard heart, that no means of grace shall have any effect upon 'em, but only to harden 'em more and more. So it was with some of those that Christ preached to. John 12:39–40, "Therefore they could not believe, because, that Esaias said again, He hath blinded their eyes, and hardened their heart; that they should not see with their eyes, nor understand with their heart, and be converted, and I should heal them."

And sinners don't know how long God's patience will be lengthened, and the day of the striving of his Spirit, before it comes to this, that he will finally leave 'em. They don't know how soon it will come to that, that God will as it were swear in his wrath that they shall never enter into his rest.

When they are tempted to commit any sin, they don't know but that is the very sin which will provoke God forever to give 'em up to sin. They don't know how many more known and willful sins God will bear with in them, before it comes to this, that he inflicts this awful judgment upon them of leaving them to judicial hardness. They don't know whether he will bear with more than one more; if they are stirred up by their lusts to another sinful action, they don't know but that will be the last.

One willful sin is a most dreadful provocation to God. And though God, it may be, sometimes has borne with those that have committed more willful sins than they, and has not given 'em up to hardness of heart, yet that is no argument that he won't give them up to such a judgment: for he acts his own sovereign pleasure in that matter. God's patience holds out longer with some than others. There are some that he is provoked to give 'em up to hardness of heart sooner than with others.

'Tis true that the gospel does reveal God's mercy to be infinite, but at the same time it reveals God's sovereignty, and that he has mercy on whom he will have mercy, and hardens whom he will, Rom. 9:18.

The gospel does reveal that if they do go on in sin, on in a way of willful sin yet longer, though it be never so much longer, that the blood of Christ will be sufficient to cleanse 'em, and that God may after all pardon 'em if he pleases, without hurting the honor of his majesty. And it reveals that there is mercy enough in God, after all, to give 'em repentance and faith in Christ: and hence they often are wont to take encouragement to go on in sin. But then they don't consider that though God can, through

Christ, convert 'em after all, without any prejudice to his glory, yet it don't follow that he will. God don't bring to Christ everyone that the blood of Christ is sufficient for.

Though God has mercy enough to give repentance, though sinners yet indulge their lusts, yet it don't follow from thence that God won't be provoked by it to refuse to give 'em repentance, because God exercises his infinite mercy according to his sovereign pleasure.

He may give repentance, and none can say that he will not, because his mercy is infinite. But he may refuse it.

The mercy of God is under the direction of the wisdom of God. And though it be true that if the sinner goes on still in sin, his mercy is sufficient to give him repentance, yet it may be agreeable to his wisdom to refuse it.

This we learn from the Word of God, that God doth often punish those that allowedly go on in known sin with a giving them up forever to sin. And we learn from thence, that a way of sinning against light, and great mercy, has a tendency to that. And therefore, 'tis most unreasonably that any take encouragement from the mercy of God to commit any more willful sin, because they don't know but one sin more will make an eternal separation between God and them, and will provoke God forever to leave them impenitent.

And especially doth this presumption on mercy tend to provoke God to deny mercy, Deut. 29:18–20. And if God don't give men repentance of sin, they are surely, as inevitably, damned. If God should be provoked by their going on in sin, still to leave them to a finally impenitent heart, it would be certain damnation, and more terrible than if it were a present damnation.

Sixth. It is unreasonable from anything in the gospel to take encouragement still to go on in sin, because the gospel gives men no assurance of the continuance of their lives. The gospel gives assurance of eternal life in case men turn from their sins while in this life, but it gives no assurance of the continuance of this life, which is the only opportunity to turn from sin.

The gospel reveals the mercy of God to be so great, that it is sufficient for old sinners as well as others, and that it is also sufficient not only to pardon old sinners upon their repentance, but that 'tis sufficient to give 'em repentance.

And many abuse this to encourage themselves to go on in sin, not considering that the gospel don't assure 'em that they shall live one day longer. If they, upon presumption of late repentance, should determine to live in sin for so much longer—suppose a year or a month—it is very unreasonable, because they don't know that they shall live a year, or month, or a week, or a day longer.

And if death should come and find us going on in sin, we should be inevitably damned. The gospel abundantly warns us of the uncertainty of the continuance of our time of probation. Christ tells us that he comes as a thief in the night. We cannot tell the day nor the hour when our Lord comes, and therefore bids us be ready, Matt. 25:13.

Christ informs us of one that blessed himself in a presumption of a long continuance in the world, that yet had his soul required of him that night, Luke 12:20.

So that the gospel not only don't give encouragement to go on in sin always, and shows the necessity of forsaking sin and living holily some time or other before we die; but neither does it give encouragement to go on in sin at all for one day, in that it don't assure any one of us of the continuance of our lives for one day to an end.

Seventh. Though the gospel reveals the mercy of God and the blood of Christ to be as sufficient for the greatest sinner as for the least, yet that don't argue but that great sinners may be more exposed to damnation than others.

Some encourage themselves from that consideration to go on in sin, and to be very wicked, to give themselves a full swing: for, say they, "Christ's blood is sufficient for the greatest sinners; the mercy of God is as sufficient for the great sinners as for others." And so {they encourage themselves, and} they argue that they shall be as likely to be saved, as if they were lesser sinners: but very unreasonably, for it don't follow that because God's mercy is as sufficient for one as for another, that therefore one is no more exposed to damnation than another, or that one is in no greater danger of missing of salvation than another.

All notwithstanding this, some sinners are in much greater danger of hell than others. Though all are in very great danger, yet some are more dreadfully exposed; some are a great deal more likely to be damned than others. It is to be considered, as we observed before, that though the mercy of God be equally sufficient for all sorts, yet God dispenses his mercy according to his wisdom and sovereign pleasure, and God may see it agreeable to his wisdom more rarely to show mercy to some than to others. [In] Mark 12:34, Christ tells one that he was not far from the kingdom of God, by which it appears that some are in a more hopeful way to be saved than others, though sinners.

So we learn by the Word of God that there are some sorts of sinners that are but rarely brought to repentance. The Wise Man speaking of the strange woman, says Prov. 2:18–19, "her house inclineth unto death, and her paths unto the dead. None that go unto her return again, neither take they hold of the paths of life." Which surely implies that they are rarely brought to repentance.

They that go great lengths in sin, they go nearer to hell and are in greater danger, and are more likely to fall into it. Satan has a greater interest in them, has a stronger possession of them, and is more likely to have them at last.

So those that continue long in ways of known sin under great light, against convictions of conscience, against many warnings and great mercies: such as these are more eminently in danger of damnation, and they are seldom brought to repentance than others. Matt. 23:33, "Ye generation of vipers, how can ye escape the damnation of hell?"

Not but that God is as able to torment them as others, for matter of power and for matter of mercy. But in his wisdom he sees it not wise, because if great and heinous sinners, and sinners against great convictions, were as likely to be saved as others, why, men's wickedness would have no restraints; men would be no more afraid of the greatest and most aggravated wickedness, than of the least. The holy commandments of God would be greatly exposed to be trampled under foot.

And so old sinners are more rarely converted than others for the same reason, and not for want of power or mercy.

And on the other hand, those sinners that strive to their utmost in all things to conform themselves to God's commands, that strive against sin and do so steadily, they are in a hopeful way to be converted: not because God can convert these easier than others, or that his mercy is more sufficient for these than others, but because he sees meet in his wisdom that it should be so, that converting grace ordinarily should be bestowed on such, and that this should be the stated way of obtaining it.

So that the gospel, with all its revelations of grace, gives no encouragement to wicked men to give themselves a swing in sin, in that they are instructed that the more they do so, the more they will expose themselves to damnation; the less likely will they be to be saved.

The gospel therefore, instead of revealing anything that tends to encourage and promote sin, it tends to restrain and curb men's lust. It shows 'em how they do the more expose themselves to wrath by every degree which they advance in wickedness, and by every willful sin which they commit; and on the other hand, gives encouragement to sinners that will strive against every sin, and at all times. Thus herein they will be in a hopeful way to obtain converting grace, and so to be saved.

Eighth. The gospel shows, more than anything else, how dreadful a punishment ungodly men are exposed to, in that God did so much to deliver men from it.

The gospel don't only teach that men do expose themselves to damnation by going on in sin, but it brings to light, more than anything else whatsoever, what a terrible thing that damnation is, and therefore is very far from encouraging in sin. The gospel tells us how great things God has done to deliver men from damnation, how great expense he has been at, how greatly the Son of God has been engaged in this affair. This discovers the dreadfulness of that misery of damnation a great deal more than the threatening of the law.

It shows that it was a very dreadful misery that men were exposed to, that God should take so much notice of it; that the Son of God should be so much concerned about it; that he should do such great unknown, unheard of things; that he should put himself so exceedingly out of the way, if I may so speak, in order to deliver them from it: such as leaving heaven and coming down, taking upon him our nature, "and became obedient unto death, even the death of the cross" [Philip. 2:7][4]—surely a dreadful misery, or [he] never would have thought it worth the while.

All these actions of the Son of God, and the concern of the Father and the Holy Ghost in the affair, show the dreadfulness of the misery of damnation a great deal more than merely telling us how dreadful it was. These great things tend to command our attention and to convince the mind, carries strong evidence with it, and to make us think with ourselves what misery was this that was so great, that the persons of the Trinity should concern themselves about it at this rate.

---

4. This is a conjectural scriptural reference for where JE drew a dash in the MS.

And now the gospel, instead of encouraging men in sin, gives men this to consider: that unless they live a holy life, they must suffer this dreadful punishment that Christ did and suffered such great things to deliver men from. If they should happen to die before they are converted, they must endure this misery. If God should be provoked by their sins, deny 'em repentance, and give 'em up to hardness of heart, they must suffer this misery. By going on in sin, they will more and more expose themselves to this misery.

Ninth. The gospel is so far from encouraging sin, that it threatens a much more dreadful punishment to them that go on in sin, than there would have been if there had been no gospel. It not only reveals more of the dreadfulness of the damnation which the law threatened, but the gospel occasions the damnations of ungodly men to be really a great deal more dreadful than otherwise it would have been. They that go to hell now, that have lived under the gospel, will go to a great deal worse hell, than if there had been no gospel. And they that go to hell from places where there is no gospel, don't go to near so dreadful a hell as those that perish from under the gospel. This Christ teaches: "Woe unto thee, Chorazin! woe unto thee, Bethsaida! for if the mighty works, which were done in you, had been done in Tyre and Sidon, they would have repented long ago in sackcloth and ashes," Matt. 11:21, etc. Surely the gospel herein is very far from being an encouragement to wickedness, when it renders the punishment of wicked men a great deal more dreadful than otherwise it would; much more dreadful than if there had been only law, and no gospel.

So that this, instead of being an encouragement to sin, is an additional restraint from sin.

Tenth. The gospel ordinarily don't keep the godly themselves from fears of hell when they have need of them. One thing which may make it seem to some that the gospel gives encouragement to sin, is that when once men are converted, the gospel assures of salvation. Let 'em commit what sin they will after that, there is no danger, but that they shall go to heaven.

This has been partly answered already, where we observed that an universal obedience was a necessary and constant attendant and fruit of faith. But it may be further answered by this: that commonly when godly men stand in need of fear of hell, to awe them and to make them careful to avoid sin, they are not out of the reach of them. The godly, though they

The Gospel No Encouragement to Sin

are indeed safe from hell, and it is impossible that they should go there, yet sometimes they stand in need of fears of hell to make 'em careful and strict to avoid sin, than otherwise they would be.

But that is only in case either of weak grace or an ill frame, and that they ordinarily have them. When persons are strong in grace, or have grace in a lively exercise, they don't need fear of hell to restrain 'em from sin; they have enough also to restrain 'em. They have better principles to restrain 'em, principles of love to God and love to godliness, a hungering and thirsting after it. And a view of the glorious reward is enough to make 'em strict and exact in obedience. At such times, if there was no such thing as hell, they would be under no temptation to allowed disobedience.

But sometimes, when grace is weak or lies asleep, and the saints are in an ill frame, they commonly need the fear of hell to restrain and curb their lusts, and make them strictly to avoid sin. And commonly at such time, they have fears of hell, and that for all the gospel.

Though the gospel declares that all that are saints are safe from hell, yet commonly saints in such cases don't know that they are safe from hell. They don't know that they are saints; they ben't able at such times to apply the assurances of the gospel to themselves.

And that, for this reason, viz., that in case of weak grace, it is difficult discerning whether there be any grace in the heart or no. When grace is great, it is easily discerned and discovered, and evidently distinguished from all that arises from natural principles. But when it is small, let you give what signs you will for persons to try themselves by, it will leave 'em uncertain whether what they have be any more than may arise from natural principles.

And so in case of an ill frame, when grace is not in exercise and corruption only is in exercise, the mere thinking of past experiences won't satisfy a man. When he is in an ill frame, he won't be able to call to mind and have an idea how it was when he had the exercises of faith and love, etc., in times past; he won't be able to have an idea of what he felt and saw in his own mind and of the spiritual experience he had. And therefore, he'll be very apt to doubt whether it was right or no, whether it was any more than what is common. And so, consequently on this, he will be afraid of hell.

So that though the promises of the gospel are absolute to all saints, yet so are things wisely ordered of him who gave the gospel, that when the saints need the fears of hell to restrain 'em from sin, they have 'em. So that the absolute promises of the gospel prove no encouragement to 'em to sin: for at such times as when they are in so ill a frame that they would be an encouragement to sin, they can't come at 'em.

Eleventh. The gospel don't only discourage sin, but it encourages the contrary, so that it promotes obedience both ways. If there were only law and no gospel, obedience would not be so much promoted as 'tis now: for the law to us in our fallen state would only terrify, but would afford no encouragement at all to obedience; no promises or encouragements would belong to us, because we could not perform perfect obedience.

The gospel encourages obedience, three ways:

1. [First,] is that it reveals that such obedience as attainable by us fallen creatures may be accepted. This is great encouragement for us to strive that we may be as obedient as possible, encouragement to strive against sin and to be exact in a conformity to God's law. Whereas, if we had no prospect of being accepted, let us do the utmost in obedience that is attainable by a fallen, corrupted creature, it would be a discouragement to us. Obedience would never be a thing so much as aimed at by us, for we should say, "Let us be as obedient as we will, and though we are never so sincere in what we do, we can't be accepted."

Now there is nothing but the gospel that reveals that our imperfect obedience may be accepted. If we had law and no gospel, we should have no prospect of being accepted in anything that it is possible for us to attain to.

2. The gospel reveals to us that we may obtain eternal life in a way of such obedience as we are capable of attaining to. If there were no gospel, the case would be desperate as to our escaping hell and obtaining eternal life. And if we despaired, we should never attempt any such thing as obedience, in whole or in part; being utterly desperate, we should have no heart to it.

But now the gospel has opened a door of hope to us, here is great encouragement for us to strive in a way of obedience. The gospel reveals that a way of universal obedience is the way to heaven. This is glorious encouragement, enough to set all upon earnestly seeking after this universal obedience.

3. The gospel reveals that no one act of sincere obedience shall miss of eternal reward. Though we have committed many sins, God will not upbraid us with them. The bad deeds of the saints shall not be set against their good deeds. But every act of sincere obedience, however small, shall

be rewarded of God to all eternity. "Whosoever shall give . . . a cup of [cold water only in the name of a disciple, verily I say unto you, he shall in no wise lose his reward]," Matt. 10:42. Now what a glorious encouragement is this to us to strive to perform as many such acts as possible, when we consider the more such we perform, the greater will our reward be, the happier shall we be to all eternity.

Now if there was only law and no gospel, we should have no encouragement to be obedient: for whatever acts of obedience we performed, it would be in vain. We should have no reward for it.

Therefore the gospel, instead of being an encouragement to sin, tends to promote obedience abundantly more than the law alone would be.

Merely the strict commands and threatenings of the law, would by no means have that tendency to promote obedience as the gospel hath with its encouragements. The law, if it were alone, would rather tend to promote sin: not through its nature, which is holy, just and good, but through our circumstances. It would work despair, and that would work death; it would not [at] all stir up to obedience, but would rather stir up to disobedience. It would do nothing but set the enmity of the heart against God into a greater rage. Rom. 7:10, "The commandment, which was ordained to life, I found to be unto death." Rom. 8:3, "What the law could not do, in that it was weak through the flesh."

Twelfth. There is nothing affords such powerful motives to ingenuity to avoid sin and obey God's commands, as the gospel doth. There is nothing that tends to attract and win the heart to obedience, [nothing that] represents the mercy and love and grace of God, [nothing that represents] what God has done for us, [than the] dying love of Christ. "[The] love of Christ constrains us, because we thus judge it," II Cor. 5:14. [It] tends to make [us] to hate sin, that it cost the Son of God so dear. [It shows] a better, a spiritual obedience. The law, if we were under that only, would have no tendency to draw, but only to drive and force, with fear and terror. But what is such a slavish, forced obedience worth, in comparison of that which is drawn by motives that draw forth the heart in love and gratitude to perform a filial obedience?[5]

---

5. End of second preaching unit. JE repeats the text and Doctrine, which are here omitted.

APPLICATION

Use I of *Instruction*

First. Hence we may see the great wisdom of God in the work of redemption, that he redeems sinners without giving any encouragement to sin. The great difficulty in the work of redemption was how sin ever should be redeemed without prejudice to any attribute, how the matter should be contrived that no attribute should have anything against it, that all the attributes might agree and conspire in this way, and go hand in hand in it; or, as the Scripture expression is, might meet together and kiss each other, Ps. 85:10.

Mercy sought the salvation of sinners, but then here was a great difficulty: how justice should allow of it. This difficulty is got out by contriving that Jesus Christ shall satisfy justice by his blood.

But then here is also a difficulty: how the holiness of God should be reconciled to it. If God provides a satisfaction for all the sins that men commit, won't God be chargeable with giving countenance and encouragement to sin, and so injure the honor of his holiness? It would not be for the honor of the holiness of God if he should be the author of any such dispensation as should tend to encourage and promote sin and wickedness. But by the Doctrine we learn that the work of redemption is so contrived, that this attribute also hath nothing against it, the gospel being no way an encouragement to sin, but the reverse of it.

It was the design of God by the gospel to show that his mercy was without bounds, sufficient for every sinner, every sort of sinner, and of every degree of wickedness. But yet, this infinite and all-sufficient mercy is dispensed in such a way, that the wicked man can find no foundation of encouragement to him to go on in sin, or to rest in it. The sufficiency of the mercy of God for him that doth as yet go on in sin, can be no just ground of ease or quietness and carelessness of spirit to any in a sinful state, so hath the wisdom of God ordered and contrived things.

It was the will of God that man should be in no part his own savior, that he should have no hand in that work of redemption, but that Christ should do all, that all the glory of redemption might belong to him. But yet so are things contrived, that this should no way encourage man in sloth and negligence of his own salvation. Though Christ be the only Redeemer, and the work of redemption be from the foundation to the topstone his work, yet so hath the wisdom of God contrived that

The Gospel No Encouragement to Sin

there should be no encouragement for men to be idle and do nothing. Notwithstanding this, men's neglecting their own salvation will be fatal; it will be their inevitable ruin. And there is a necessity of man's care of his own salvation and diligence in seeking of it, in order to his being saved.

So [it] is the will of God that the salvation of men should be owing only to the righteousness of Christ, and that men's own righteousness and obedience and good works should have nothing to do in his justification; that Christ should do all, that he should obey the law in the stead of sinners, that he should have righteousness enough, without any obedience or righteousness of theirs. And yet, for all this, so hath divine wisdom ordered things, that here is no encouragement for men to neglect being righteous and obeying the law themselves. Yea, there is a necessity of their truly and sincerely endeavoring to be righteous in all things, notwithstanding.

There is none of the glory of men's salvation that is to be ascribed to men themselves, but all to God; nothing of it is to be ascribed to men's own righteousness. And yet, so are matters ordered, that there is great encouragement to men to be righteous themselves, to seek an inherent righteousness. They shall, notwithstanding, have set before them a prospect of great honors and glory in reward for their sincere righteousness.

So wonderfully hath the wisdom of God contrived and ordered [things], that there is no encouragement in it to sin, either to those that are already interested in redemption, or those that are not. Those that are, as yet, interested in Christ's redemption, they have it offered to 'em freely; they may have it at any time, only upon a hearty acceptance of it, without any works of their own. And yet, for all this, the gospel affords great matter of terrors to 'em if they go on in sin, and neglect works of righteousness.

And concerning those that are already interested in redemption, the gospel absolutely promises salvation to 'em. It is impossible they should anyway miss of it. And yet, so are matters ordered, that here is no door opened for them from hence to take a liberty to indulge themselves in their lusts.

So hath the wisdom of God manifested itself in the ordering of this. Though the gospel be so full of discoveries of the infinite and free mercy of God to sinners, and to the greatest sinners, yet there can be nothing in the world contrived or thought of that would tend so much discourage and suppress sin and wickedness, and promote obedience, as the gospel doth.

Second. Hence learn how unreasonable wicked men are, that take encouragement to sin from what the gospel reveals to us. How commonly is this the case. Are there not some now here present that live wicked lives, neglecting the known duties of religion, and that sin in many instances against their light, and are in a great measure easy and secure in such a way?

And the thing which they encourage and embolden themselves by, is this: that the Scriptures teach that God is infinitely merciful, and so they hope that God will have mercy on them, notwithstanding. They hope God won't refuse to show 'em mercy, though they do sin very grievously in the way that they are in. And they hope God will have mercy on 'em—though they go on in sin yet a long time—if then they set themselves to pray to God for mercy. Yea, they hope if they should spend their whole lives in sin, they may prevail upon mercy to pity 'em and save 'em on their deathbeds.

And so they flatter themselves with that, [that] Christ has suffered enough to satisfy for their sins, let 'em sin never so much. They encourage themselves that sometimes the chief of sinners are saved, them that have been a great deal more wicked than they, and that mercy is offered to all. If they should live in a way of neglect of secret prayer, or in a way of intemperance, or a way of lasciviousness and gratifying of their sensual lusts this long time, mercy would be offered to 'em still.

I desire those that are here present, that do allow themselves in such ways as these, to inquire whether it is not thus with them. What is it that emboldens you to do as you do? There is doubtless something or other that you flatter yourself with. Is it not such a presumption on mercy as we have spoke of? Don't you abuse the revelation that the gospel makes of free grace to this purpose?

But then, how little do you consider what a revelation the gospel makes of the justice as well as of the mercy of God, that though God has declared that he is gracious and merciful, longsuffering, abundant in goodness and truth, "forgiving iniquity, transgression and sin," yet he has also, at the same time, declared that he "will by no means clear the guilty" [Ex. 34:7].

You don't consider what the gospel doth so abundantly manifest, viz., how impossible it is that any one sin should go without its due

The Gospel No Encouragement to Sin

punishment, how dreadful God's hatred of sin is and how terrible his wrath towards it, and how inflexible his justice in revenging it; and consequently, how dreadful your punishment would be if you should at last be found with the guilt of sin upon you, and how impossible that you should escape.

You don't sufficiently consider how impossible it is, for all the infiniteness of mercy, that ever you should be converted and saved, unless you do wholly renounce all known sin and mortify every lust. You little consider how uncertain it is, whether ever God will give you repentance of your sins and give you faith in Christ, and how much you expose yourself by every step you take in allowed sinning, to that judgment and curse of God, of being forever left of God to a hard and impenitent heart: and that, notwithstanding of all that the gospel reveals about the mercy of God and the satisfaction of Christ. You very much misunderstand the gospel, if you think there is anything at all in it that gives you any kind of intimation that you shall hereafter have repentance given you, though you yet go on in sin. The gospel is wholly silent about [this], and there is nothing in it that you can so much as draw it from; there is not the least encouragement of any such thing. And if you take encouragement and expect that God will hereafter give you repentance, you merely presume upon it, of your own head. God gives you none; the gospel affords none.

And if you think you are in no greater danger of hell for your giving yourself such a swing in gratifying your own carnal inclinations than others that live moral and orderly lives, or if you think you shall be no more likely to be damned next year than you are now or tomorrow, than you are today, though you yet go on in sin: it is a vain imagination of yours. If you argue it from that, that the mercy of God and redemption of Christ will be as sufficient for you then as it is now, you draw a false inference. Though the mercy of God and Christ's blood be alike sufficient for all, it doth not at all follow from thence that great sinners are in no more danger than lesser ones, or that you don't more and more expose yourself to hell the more sin you commit, as we have shown.

You don't sufficiently consider how little assurance you have of the continuance of your life, how uncertain you are, but that your soul this night be required of you.

You take encouragement to go on in sin, because God reveals his infinite mercy and offers pardon for sinners. But do you consider that, by going on in sin, you expose yourself to a damnation that is much more dreadful than if there never had been any revelation of mercy or any offer of pardon at all?

You ben't at all assured of having the benefit of that mercy, and by every willful sin you commit, you bring yourself still into greater danger of failing of it. And then, if you do fail of it, it will be manifoldly worse for you than if Christ never had died for sinners. The infinite mercy of God in Christ will do you no good, but it will only be an occasion of a much more terrible destruction. The Doctrine teaches us how unreasonable they are that, thinking themselves to be in a converted state, encourage themselves in sin from the absoluteness of the promises of eternal life that are made to such, and are wont to make their hopes a pillow for the indulgence of carnal sloth.

These don't sufficiently consider the text, which tells us that we build again the things that we destroyed. We make ourselves transgressors, or prove ourselves yet to be in sin, if we still go on to build what we seemed by faith and repentance to destroy.

They don't consider the nature of true faith, that there is implied in it a mortification of the principle of sin and the heart's renouncing of the ways of sin, and that true faith is of a working nature. It works by love, and shows its nature by obedience, as the root shows its nature by the fruit which it bears.

They ben't sensible that it is as truly necessary in order to salvation, that the life that persons live ben't a wicked but a holy, obedient life, as if obedience were the proper condition of salvation.

Use II of *Expostulation*. I would ask those that are careless in sin, If it be so, as we have now heard, that the gospel gives no encouragement to sin, what does? There is something in the foundation of that ease and security that you live in, is most manifest, whether it be a just foundation, or a foundation that has any strength; yet doubtless, there is something that your carelessness is built on. The nature of every man is equally averse from misery. Therefore, seeing that you often hear of a hell, of eternal misery that you and we all are naturally exposed to, there must be something that is the foundation of your quietness and carelessness with respect to that misery, that keeps you so easy about it, that you can concern yourself so little about any means of deliverance, that you can go up and down amongst men so cheerful, that you can eat and drink with a merry heart and rest quietly in your beds: and not only so, but go on daily provoking of God in ways that you know his Word disallows of.

If the gospel affords no just foundation for this security and carelessness, what is it that it is built upon?

First. Does the law give you any encouragement? Though you can't find any just ground of encouragement in the gospel, do you imagine you see it in the law? Do you find any promises there that you think applicable to such as you are?

This gives no encouragement to you; by this you are condemned. If you had no other sin than only what you bring into the world with you, much more when, to your original, you have added so many actual sins as you have done.

In the law you find nothing but condemnation and curses denounced against you, which cries "cursed is everyone that confirms not all the words of this law to do them," Deut. 27:26.[6] By this, you are condemned to eternal death for every sin you commit. "The wages of sin is death," Rom. 6:23.

The law condemns you as it were to a new death for every new sinful act or thought that you are guilty [of] in the whole course of your life. And 'tis an eternal death that is the wages of every sin.

Second. Does reason or the light of nature give you any encouragement?

Here consider:

1. Reason and the light of nature afford no ground to hope that there is no future eternal punishment. Nay, reason abundantly confirms it that there is. The doctrine of the Word of God concerning these things is a most rational doctrine. Reason doth abundantly teach that there is a God; that he that is our Creator must be our rightful King [and] lawgiver; that it belongs to him to give us laws to govern ourselves by, and to enforce; that [he] has given us our reason, that we govern ourselves according to reason, according to the natures that he has given us; [that he] must be offended when we act unjustly or contrary to the natures that he has given us.

Some things must be pleasing to him, and others offensive. [It] must be offensive for us to hate him, to contemn our Creator, and improve our faculties and enjoyments which he, of his goodness, has given us, as weapons of warfare against him, because unreasonable.

---

6. "'Not all the words of this law to do them,' Deut. 27:26,'" is a later addition.

And if something, some kinds of actions in [us], be offensive and displeasing to God, then 'tis most rational to suppose that, seeing he is our King, that he should forbid them. If some things in a subject are offensive to God, who is by right our sovereign Lord and lawgiver, then surely 'tis rational to suppose that he should give us a law wherein these things should be forbidden. And if God doth give us a law, 'tis most rational to suppose that he will enforce his law with threatenings of punishment. There is no law without [it]. Merely to forbid, without giving any ground to expect punishment, is for the lawgiver, and him that forbids, only to ex[pose] himself and his authority to contempt. A law without a sanction, is no law at all.

[It is] rational to suppose that these punishments should be in a measure proportionable to the greatness and majesty of the lawgiver, his displeasure proportionably dreadful, [his] law proportionably sacred, and our obligations to obey him proportionable to the heinousness of the offense of disobeying him.

[It is rational to suppose that God's] greatness and majesty, [which are] infinite, [are proportionable to the] infinite distance between him and us.

[Our] obligation [is] infinite, [as God is] infinitely worthy in himself. Therefore, [a] crime [against God is] infinitely heinous. Therefore, [the] punishment [is] infinite. Reason plainly teaches [this].

Reason teaches that wickedness [receives its] punishment in a future world. [It is] not punished in this world.

Thus, reason affords you no help at all. It confirms what the Word of God teaches of a future punishment, and of the dreadfulness and eternity of it, and that your punishment will be proportionably dreadful to the number and heinousness and aggravations of your sins. [Even the] heathens, many of 'em, believed [thus].

2. Whether there be any future eternal punishment or no, yet reason teaches you the folly of going on in a way of allowed sinning, unless you are sure there is not.

Because an eternal misery is an infinite evil. If there be any such thing, it is a thing infinitely to be dreaded, when one dies, to fall into the hands of enraged Omnipotence, to be tormented by him without the least pity; and to be tormented by devils, to dwell in a furnace of fire, and there to have inexpressible torment every moment, day and night, without one moment's respite, and without any hope or possibility of deliverance or

The Gospel No Encouragement to Sin

end, forever and ever. And seeing it is so great an evil, reason teaches that is folly to put ourselves into, or voluntarily to continue in such circumstances, wherein there is any room for suspicion of falling into such misery. Reason teaches us to be more cautious of greater calamities, than of lesser ones. As for those sufferings that are light and trivial, reason will allow of one not being much concerned about them, but teaches it to be our prudence to be very cautious of very great calamities.

Reason teaches us more to dread and avoid a probability, or even the possibility, of some evils, than the certainty of others, and that, even in temporal evils, because some are so much more dreadful than others. And above all does reason teach it to be our prudence to avoid, so far as we can, so much as a possibility of an infinite evil, or to avoid exposing ourselves to an infinite possible evil.

And especially, when we expose ourselves to that evil by doing what is ill and unreasonable in itself. A wise man would run a far greater venture in doing well, than in doing ill.

Therefore, whether there be a hell or not, reason teaches it to be folly in persons allowedly to go on in sin, as long as they don't know but that there is, as long as they don't know but that all that the Word of God teaches about it is true. And if it be thus, their so doing as they do is likely to be infinitely to their cost.

I would therefore put it to such persons, if any be here present, that flatter themselves with hopes that there will not prove to be such a hell as the Scriptures tell us of and fright us with, that [it] is nothing but [a] mere scarecrow, and so hence embolden themselves to go on in sin: I would ask them whether ever they thoroughly examined and inquired into that matter, so as to come to good assurance that there is not.

How do you know but that what the Scripture says about it [is] true? And if you don't know, why will you rest in such a dreadful uncertainty? You are altogether uncertain whether there be a hell or no; and if there be one, you are certain of that, that the way you are now in, you shall go to it.

If it should prove at last that there is one, will you not accuse yourself of great folly, that you trusted to that of which you was so uncertain?

3. Reason teaches that (if there be a hell), the longer you continue in sin and the more sin you commit, the more you are exposed to it.

'Tis unreasonable to suppose that an infinitely-wise God would order it any otherwise. For if a man be not at all the more likely to be damned, let him be as wicked as he will, and continue to sin as long as he will, here is a door opened for all manner of licentiousness: then he that governs the world has so ordered the matter, that he has very much left the wickedness of the world without restraint.

4. Reason affords no assurance of the continuance of your opportunity to escape hell. The gospel gives no assurance of this, so neither does reason. But it teaches from the experience of all nations and ages, that no man is certain of the continuance of life; that no man, whether sick or in health, is certain of the continuance of life one day to another; that death commonly comes suddenly, seldom comes expected, [and] often comes when least expected.

Therefore, if the foundation of your security be this, that you flatter yourself that you shall live long and opportunity enough to forsake your sins and turn to God hereafter, you act very unreasonably.

5. Reason teaches that misery is not at all the less to be avoided, because it is in a future and unseen world. If that be what is the foundation of your security, that the torments of hell ben't present—they are, for ought you know, a great way off, you feel nothing of 'em at present—how unreasonably do you act, as if the misery that begins forty or fifty years hence, won't be as intolerable when it comes, as if it began now. Is this a rational ground of fearlessness of eternal torments, that it may possibly be some years before they begin?

Or are you secure, because hell at present is out of sight? How little do you act like a rational creature herein, how much like a child as rather than a reasonable being, as if hell were not in itself so dreadful, because at present you don't see nor feel how dreadful it is, however terrible it is represented to your reason!

6. Reason again teaches that you are not the less foolish in your security and carelessness, because many others are so too. Is this what you make a ground of your being so quiet in neglecting your soul, that you see that a great many others are careless? Are you the less foolish for running headlong into hellfire, because you see that is the course that the multitudes take? By considering of these things, you will see that you don't act like men, that you don't act as if you had the use of a faculty of understanding, but that you turn to your own way, "as the horse rusheth [into battle]," Jer. 8:6, and that you are as the horse and the mule, "[which have no understanding]," Ps. 32:9.[7]

---

7. The remainder of the sermon, which has been formatted as a final Use, is outlined, recapitulating the first and second main heads of the Doctrine, upon which JE doubtless

[*Use* III.]

First. Things that sinners abuse to this purpose.⁸

1. [The gospel reveals the] infinite mercy [of God].

2. [The gospel reveals how] Christ suffered enough [to satisfy for the sins of all mankind].

3. [The gospel reveals that there is] no need of our righteousness [for our justification].

4. [The gospel offers] pardon and salvation offered to all.

5. [The gospel offers] absolute promises of salvation to converted ones.

Second. [The gospel is] no encouragement [to sin].

1. Every sin [is] as much forbidden. [We are] under greater obligations [to obedience].

2.⁹ [The] gospel more fully reveals the duties of moral law.

3. [The gospel] more fully [reveals] the terribleness of [God's] wrath, and [his] strictness and justice in punishing [sin].

4. [The gospel reveals the] necessity of universal obedience.

5. [The gospel gives] no assurance of giving repentance.

6. [The gospel gives] no assurance of continuance of life.

7. [The gospel reveals that] great sinners [are] more exposed to damnation [than others].

8. [The] gospel shows, more than anything, how dreadful a punishment wicked men are exposed to.

9. [The] punishment will actually be great.

[10.] It don't keep [the] godly from fears, when needed.

11. [The gospel] gives encouragement [to obedience].

[(1)] [It reveals that] attainable obedience may be accepted.

[(2)] [It reveals that the way of obedience] is the way to life.

[(3)] [It reveals that] every act shall be rewarded.

12. [There is nothing that affords such powerful] motives to ingenuity [to avoid sin and obey God's commands].

---

would have extemporized.

8. The points here are reiterations of those under the first and second heads of the Doctrine, respectively; doubtless JE expanded on each point extemporaneously.

9. MS: "3." The subsequent points under this head are consequently misnumbered as well.

FLESH AND SPIRIT
(Gal. 5:17, 1745)

IN ONE OF HER POEMS, THE EARLY SEVENTEENTH-CENTURY NEW England writer Anne Bradstreet created an allegorical conversation between *The Flesh and the Spirit*. After Flesh has chided Spirit for seeking that which cannot be seen while there is so much to enjoy below, Spirit begins her reply:

> Be still thou unregenerate part,
> Disturb no more my setled heart,
> For I have vow'd, (and so will doe)
> Thee as a foe, still to pursue.
> And combat with thee will and must,
> Untill I see thee laid in th' dust.
> Sisters we are, ye[a] twins we be,
> Yet deadly feud 'twist thee and me.

For a sermonic depiction of the relation of these "twins," Edwards too uses the language of combat, of "inward struggle," saying, dramatically, that there is "nothing else like it to be found in the universe." He likens flesh and spirit to corruption and grace, two "principles" in the human nature. Edwards begins by providing scripture proofs of the reality of human corruption, much as he does later in the opening section of *The Great Christian Doctrine of Original Sin Defended*, describing how, in "original righteousness," superior principles regulated the inferior principles, but that this order was upset with the fall. In the Application, he explores the nature of the opposition between these two principles in saints and in sinners, pointing to the manner of opposition as being a key difference. The opposition to the flesh, or corruption, in sinners is only "partial"; they "seek just so much religion as they think will carry 'em to heaven." In saints, however, this opposition is located not merely in the reason or conscience, but in the heart. The Spirit, indwelling there, helps them to "overcome."

Sermon Notebook "45" is one of several surviving manuscripts in which Edwards jotted down ideas for sermons, including this one. His original notation for this sermon reads, "Show the difference between this and the struggle of natural conscience with corruption."[1] While grace is the "victorious" principle over corruption, Edwards does allow that natural conscience can work with grace in overcoming sin and temptation, but it cannot do so alone and perseveringly in the absence of grace. These distinctions hark back to "Miscellanies" nos. 471–72, which discuss the different ways the Spirit of God works upon the hearts of converted and natural individuals (*WJE* 13:512–14).

Edwards does some interesting things here with the façade of the sermon form, if not the form itself. The Exposition is presented as four *Observations* with a *Reason*, and what is the doctrinal section begins with a "Subject" and a statement of "Method." Possibly, Edwards was trying to give a slightly more modern turn to his sermonic presentation.

Edwards deals in other writings with the theme of "flesh" and "spirit," including *Original Sin*,[2] sermon fifteen of "Charity and Its Fruits,"[3] the Miscellanies,[4] and the "Treatise on Grace."[5] Last but not least, Edwards

---

1. *WJE* 36 Sermon Notebook 45 (W5.0), "[465]. Gal. The Flesh Lusteth against the sp. shew the difference between this & the struggle of natural Conscience with Corruption."

2. *WJE* 3:280, "If by 'flesh' is meant man's nature, as he receives it in his first birth, then 'therein dwelleth no good thing'; as appears by Romans 7:18. 'Tis wholly opposite to God, and to subjection to his law, as appears by Romans 8:7–8. 'Tis directly contrary to true holiness, and wholly opposes it, and holiness is opposite to that; as appears by Galatians 5:17."

3. *WJE* 8:389, "The strife and struggle of the new man is after holiness. The heart struggles after it. The heart of a good man, one who has an interest in heaven, and has an inward active, heavenly seed in him, is in a struggle with sin, as Jacob was with Esau in Rebecca's womb."

4. *WJE* 18:143, 234.

5. *WJE* 21:192. Chapter III, "Showing How a Principle of Grace Is from the Spirit of God."

Sermons by Jonathan Edwards on the Epistle to the Galatians

committed a lengthy entry on the text in the "Blank Bible,"[6] ending with an elaborate exposition in three *Corollaries*.[7]

* * * * *

The manuscript is twenty-four duodecimo-sized leaves, dated "septem. 1745" by Edwards on the top of the front page. A shorthand notation beneath the date indicates the sermon was repreached, though the location is indecipherable. Leaves two through four appear to be a dislocation, possibly a rewritten Application for that unidentifiable repreaching, stitched into the booklet at the wrong place. The text of these leaves is presented as an appendix to the sermon.

---

6. For example, see the following entries in the "Blank Bible" (*WJE* 24:927, 1008, 1038, 1067, and 1180, respectively):

John 3:6.] See notes on Galatians 5:17, the first *Corol.*

Rom 8:1.] As to the meaning of the words, "flesh" and "Spirit" here and in the context, see notes on Galatians 5:17.

1 Corinthians 2:14–15.] See notes on Galatians 5:17, especially the last paragraph before the corollaries.

1 Corinthians 15:44–45.] See notes on Galatians 5:17, *Corol.* 3.

1 Peter 4:6.] See notes on Galatians 5:17.

7. *WJE* 24:1085–90.

Flesh and Spirit

GALATIANS 5:17

For the flesh lusteth against the spirit, and the spirit against the flesh: and these are contrary the one to the other.

THE GREAT THING WHICH THE APOSTLE HAD BEEN INSISTING ON WITH the Galatians, from the beginning of the epistle, was that they should hold fast those principles and practices which are agreeable to the gospel dispensation. "Stand fast therefore in the liberty wherewith Christ hath made us free, and be not entangled again with the yoke of bondage" [Gal. 5:1].

Here in this context, he warns that they don't misinterpret and abuse this liberty, as though it consisted in licentiousness, or a liberty given to their lusts, intimating that though they live under [a] dispensation of liberty, yet the dispensation they live under does in no wise tend to encourage and promote sin; inasmuch as though it delivers men from that legal, servile principle of fear, yet it introduces another, which is evangelical, viz., love, that does more effectually tend to prevent their walking after their lusts, and to promote the fulfilling of the law of God, than that legal principle of fear, vv. 13–14.

The gospel is a dispensation of the Spirit {of God}, but this evangelical principle of divine love is the special fruit of the Spirit; and therefore the Apostle[1] adds in the verse before the text: "[This I say then, Walk in the Spirit, and ye shall not fulfill the lust of the flesh]."

---

1. LL. 1–2 are made from a fragment of a letter from Stephen Williams to JE, dated Mar. 20 [1745?]; see Letter B044, *WJEO* 32.

If you follow this principle of divine love, the special fruit of the Spirit, it will prevent your abusing your being licentious and giving the loose to your lusts, under a notion of Christian liberty. What is said in the text is to confirm this, viz., to show that if they walk in the Spirit, they shall not fulfill the lusts of the flesh. This the Apostle confirms from the greatness of the opposition there is between the flesh and the spirit.

Observation 1. What are the things which the Apostle here speaks of as opposing one another, flesh and spirit.

By which is plainly meant the same as grace and corruption, as appears by what follows: "Now the works of the flesh are manifest, which are these; Adultery, fornication, uncleanness, lasciviousness, idolatry, witchcraft, hatred, variance, emulations, wrath, strife, seditions, heresies, envyings, murders, drunkenness, revellings, and such like: of the which I tell you before, as I have also told you in time past, that they which do such things shall not inherit the kingdom of God. But the fruit of the Spirit is love, joy, peace, longsuffering, gentleness, goodness, faith, meekness, temperance: against such there is no law" [vv. 19–23]. And the use of those words in other places. John 3:5–6, "Verily I say [unto thee], Except a man be born of water and of the Spirit, he cannot enter into the kingdom of God. That which is born of the flesh is flesh; and that which is born of the Spirit is spirit." Rom. 7:5, "For when we were in the flesh, the motions of sins, which were by the law, did work in our members to bring forth fruit unto death"; v. 18, "For I know that in me (that is, in my flesh,) dwelleth no good thing: for to will is present with me; but how to perform that which is good I find not." Rom. 8:5, etc., "For they that are after the flesh do mind the things of the flesh; but they that are after the Spirit the things of the Spirit. For to be carnally minded is death; but to be spiritually minded is life and peace. Because the carnal mind is enmity against God: for it is not subject to the law of God, neither indeed can be. So then they that are in the flesh cannot please God. But ye are not in the flesh, but in the Spirit, if so be that the Spirit of God dwell in you. Now if any man have not the Spirit of Christ, he is none of his."

The *Reason* why corrupt nature is called flesh. Human nature [is] often called flesh. Gen. 6:12, "And God looked upon the earth, and, behold, it was corrupt; for all flesh had corrupted his way upon the earth." Ps. 65:2, [O thou that] hearest prayer, unto thee shall all flesh come. Is. 40:5–6, "And the glory of the Lord shall be revealed, and all flesh shall see it together: for the mouth of the Lord hath spoken it. The voice said, Cry.

And he said, What shall I cry? All flesh is grass, and all the goodliness thereof is as the flower of the field"; and 49:26, "And I will feed them that oppress thee with their own flesh; and they shall be drunken with their own blood, as with sweet wine: and all flesh shall know that I the Lord am thy Savior and thy Redeemer, the mighty One of Jacob"; and 66:16, "For by fire and by his sword will the Lord plead with all flesh: and the slain of the Lord shall be many." Matt. 24:22, "[And except those days should be shortened,] no flesh should be saved: but for the elect's sake those days shall be shortened." John 1:14, "The word was made flesh, and dwelt among us, (and we beheld his glory, the glory as of the only begotten of the Father,) full of grace and truth."

Grace is called spirit.[2]

Observation 2. The opposition is mutual.

Observation 3. The manner of it. "[Flesh] lusteth [against the spirit]."

Observation 4. The reason of it.

THE SUBJECT IS,

That inward mutual opposition and strife that there between grace and corruption in the heart of the saints, during their continuance in this world.

METHOD

I. There are these two principles, of grace and corruption, subsisting together.

II. What a mutual opposition and strife there is between these in the hearts of the saints during their continuance in this world.

III. Give the reasons of it.

IV. Observe some of the effects of it.

I. I would observe that there are these two principles, of grace and corruption, in the hearts of all the saints, while in this world.

[Corruption is] the most eminent. I Kgs. 8:46, "there is no man that sinneth not." Job 9:1–3, "Then Job answered and said, I know it is so of a truth: but how should man be just with God? If he will contend with him,

---

2. Variant: "Spirit." Perhaps JE had in mind a text such as Heb. 10:29, which speaks of the "Spirit of grace."

he cannot answer him one of a thousand." V. 26, "They are passed away as the swift ships: as the eagle that hasteth to the prey." Ps. 19:12–13, "Who can understand his errors? [cleanse thou me from secret faults. Keep back thy servant also from presumptuous sins; let them not have dominion over me: then shall I be upright, and I shall be innocent from the great transgression]." Ps. 130:3, "If thou, Lord, shouldst mark iniquity, [O Lord, who shall stand]?" Prov. 20:9, "Who can say, I have made my heart clean, I am pure from my sin?" Eccles. 7:20, "For there is not a just man, [that doeth good, and sinneth not]." Jas. 3:2, "In many things we offend all." I John 1:8, "If we say we have no sin, we deceive [ourselves, and the truth is not in us]." Scripture examples [show that the principle of corruption is eminent].

These opposite principles subsist together in the same heart. They don't reign together, but they have a being together in the same heart, in the same faculties—understanding [and] will—and both appear in the same affections of the soul, [such as] love.

The principles are together, and in many respects the exercises are also together. The exercises are very much mixed one with another in different acts of the soul. Though the acts are different and opposite, yet [they are] much mixed, one closely following another. Exercises of corruptions [are] mixed with the highest exercises of grace. [They are] mixed in the same prosecution of the same affair and business, and the same duties. Yea, they are joined together in the very same individual acts of the soul.

Gracious acts [are] in some respect corrupt acts, as corruption has some influence upon them; [they are] all defectively corrupt. [They are] no more humble: that is through the influence of remaining pride. [They have] no more love: {that is through} remaining enmity. [They are] no more heavenly.

Here, this *Inquiry* may be raised now: How this came to pass, that the saints should have both these principles thus joined together in their hearts.

[There is] something very mysterious in it; as it appeared strange to Rebecca that children should struggle together and oppose one another, that were together in the same womb. Gen. [25:22], "If it be so, [why am I thus]?"

Therefore, for the better understanding of this matter, these four things may be considered:

First. That man in his first estate had only holy principles.

Indeed, {man} had other principles than those, wherein his holiness did properly and immediately consist.[3]

Second. Man by his rebellion lost all his holy principles, and then had only corrupt principles.

[This is the] reason why corruption [is] called "flesh," [and] called "natural."

Third. Christ by his redemption purchased that man should have corrupt principles removed, that he might have only holy principles again.

Fourth. God, for the more evident display of his perfections in this great [affair], is pleased to order that his great work of taking away {corrupt principles} and restoring {holy principles}, should be done gradually.

[This is] the greatest of all the works of God. 'Tis for the more sensible display of his power to our finite minds, that this work should be wrought by many steps. [So the] work of creation, overthrow[ing] Satan's kingdom in the world, and setting up [Christ's kingdom].

'Tis for the greater display of his wisdom. He is pleased to use means. Wisdom appears in the ordering these means for the gradual accomplishing this great work: wonderfully defeating Satan, marvelously conducting saints through the difficulties, making his power manifest in weakness, causing things to work in an unexpected and surprising manner, bringing good out of evil, appearing in the greatest intricacies. [So it was with the] work of creation, [the] redemption out of Egypt, giving possession of Canaan, casting out the heathen, calling of the gentiles, [and] setting up the kingdom of Christ in the world.

[In this manner we have the] more clear and sensible display of the grace of God. [And it is made known] to us in a more sensible and more affecting manner.

['Tis] for the greater glory of the Mediator, [and to show] the more abundant experience of our dependence on him. Hereby, he is of the greater use. ['Tis an] occasion to bring their dependence the more abundantly into view.

['Tis] for the greater triumph over God's enemies, for the greater baffling and confusion of God's enemies. They have a long opportunity to exert themselves, [and] try all ways.

---

3. LL. 7–8 are made from a fragment of a letter from Samuel Hopkins to JE, dated March 29, 1744; see Letter B40, *WJEO* 32.

Fifth. 'Tis agreeable to the design of the present and future state, that this great work should not be brought to perfection till[4] the saints leave this world.

II. To show what a mutual strife and opposition there is between those principles in the hearts of the saints.

['Tis] typified [in the] struggle between Esau and Jacob [Gen. 25:22], Israel and the Canaanites, [the] house of Saul and the house of David.

Here, the following things may be observed concerning the nature of this strife:

First. 'Tis by lusting one against another.

Opposition is often the manner of opposite inclination, concerning natural appetites.

There is nothing else like it to be found in the universe: two natures, working and exerting themselves one against another.

Second. 'Tis very great.

['Tis] implied in the words "lusting" [and] "strong desires." Scriptures do abundantly represent there to be a very great and vigorous warfare between the saints and their spiritual enemies. The work of a Christian [is] represented as a great strife.

['Tis] represented by the great struggle there was of old, between the Canaanites {and the people of Israel, and between the} house of Saul {and the house of David}.

Third. {'Tis} continual.

Not that it is sensible every moment, but yet it may be said to be continual, as 'tis maintained as the exercise of their[5] lives. [So saints] hold on their way, run with patience the race before them.

And if religion be their constant business, it must needs follow that their opposition to {corrupt principles} is their constant exercise. These internal exercises of the saints will not be idle, {but} will be daily. They are like the devil, their father [John 8:44]. And it is the Christian's daily exercise to resist 'em.

Never is any truce made between grace and sin. Whenever either of 'em are in exercise, they oppose the contrary.

Fourth. They are irreconcilable in their opposition.

---

4. MS: "tis."
5. MS: "the."

These principles remain both together, as long as the saints continue {in this world}. They don't utterly extinguish one another, and there can be no agreement between them. As it is said, "What concord hath Christ with Belial?" [II Cor. 6:15]; so may it be said much more, What concord hath Christ and grace with sin in the abstract? There never can be any peace. The enmity is inveterate. [There is] no more possibility of any reconciliation, than between God and the devil; yea, it is in its own nature much more impossible.

III. Reasons.

They[6] are principles that are exceeding contrary one to another.

As 'tis said in the text, there is so great an opposition between no other two things in heaven or earth, as is between holiness and sin. ['Tis] greater than between light and darkness: for here, one is only a negation of the other. ['Tis] greater than between heat and cold, [or] sweet and bitter. Herein does mainly consist the opposition.[7]

APPLICATION

Use I of *Examination* {to professed believers}, whether they experience within 'em this inward opposition and strife between {corrupt and holy principles}.

Thus [it is] with all true saints.

Here I would observe, that as there is nothing in the saints but that there is a counterfeit of it in {natural men}, so there is something in many natural men that resembles and is often mistaken {for a sign of a true saint}: and that is an opposition and strife between natural conscience and lust.

[These] struggles may be very great. So [it was] in the young man, when {Jesus told him to go and sell all that he had [Matt. 19:17–22]}. [So it was] in Saul, {when he} forced himself [to offer a sacrifice, I Sam. 13:12]. [And so it was in] Naaman the Syrian, II Kgs. 5:18; [in] Herod [Matt. 14]; [and in] Felix [Acts 24:24–25].

The difference [between true saints and natural men lies in the] difference in the manner of opposition.

---

6. JE numbered this head "1," but there are no more corresponding heads before the Application.

7. This point marks the end of the first preaching unit; JE wrote the text of the sermon at the top of L. 13v. to signal the beginning of the next unit.

First. 'Tis the opposition of reason, but not the opposition of the heart.

In the strife that is between grace and corruption {in} the heart, conscience is not diverse from the faculty of reason; it is no other than the judgment of reason, as subject to the judgment of God.

This faculty is good; ['tis] the same in saints and sinners. This, so far as it is in exercise, makes opposition.

Sinners' reason declares to 'em the unrighteousness and unreasonableness there is in sin, and the evil consequences of it. But the hearts of sinners do not oppose; {they} don't comply with the voice of reason {in this strife}. But in saints, ['tis otherwise].

Second. In the opposition of one nature to another, the opposition sinners make {against corrupt principles} from conscience is all a force against nature.

'Tis not by lusting or natural appetite, [and 'tis with] fear [but] not abhorrence.

Third. In the opposition sinners seem to make to their corruption, sin is not opposed on its own account, but something else that is joined to sin; but in the saints, the opposition is against sin itself, for its own sake.

Indeed conscience, that is God's vicegerent in the soul, does oppose sin itself. But I speak of the opposition sinners make from conscience, as stirred up by conscience.

They regard the dictates of conscience no further than so as to oppose the consequences of sin. The opposition of their will is not against [the indulgence of their lusts].

Fourth. In that opposition there is in the saints between grace and corruption, sin is disallowed universally.

All sin [is disallowed], according as light is held forth. Every kind of corruption [is disallowed]: sensuality, malice, envy, revenge, evil-speaking.

[The saint will] oppose the violation of all commands, [of both the] first and second tables, [and] in all places: [in] families as well as abroad, [in] secret as well as open; [commands] of the tongue as well as hands.

[The saints will oppose] little sins as well as great, inward as well as outward; not only overt acts of sin, but the sin of the heart: this is especially meant. [The saint] opposes not only the sins of the tongue [and] hands, but the bitter root within: pride, covetousness, hypocrisy, slothfulness, blindness, stupidity.

Flesh and Spirit

[The] *Reason* appears from what was said before, {viz., they} oppose sin on its own account.

But the opposition of natural men against sin is but partial; not on its own account, or because it has the nature of sin, but for by-ends. And therefore sin is opposed no further than to obtain those by-ends, so far as to quiet conscience, [and] seek just so much religion as they think will be sufficient to carry 'em to heaven. If they can but go to heaven, they will carry as much sin with them as is possible, so much as to keep alive their hope; or if more, 'tis still for some by-ends, [to] maintain their credit [or] some worldly interest.

[They secretly retain] more gross sins, while little, overt acts of sin {they avoid, as} sins that have been much testified against.

Corruption is never opposed universally. But {sinners} oppose one corruption to gratify another; [they] pull down one idol to set up another: for all that natural men do in religion, is from a regard to some idol.

Fifth. In the opposition that is {in the heart of the saint}, sin is not only opposed universally, but it is opposed utterly.

[The] whole soul opposes, with all the faculties of mind and body: understanding, will, affections, strength.

But in that opposition that is in sinners, [it is] not so; {sin is not opposed universally}. Reason [is involved], but not the will; [they oppose sin] with some affections, but not with others; with fear, but not with abhorrence. [They make] some faint wishes and prayers, but not with their strength.

In that opposition that there is between grace {and corruption in the heart of a saint}, sin is opposed as an enemy that is hated. {But in} sinners, {corruption is} opposed not as an enemy, but as a friend of necessity. As one that is a secret traitor to his prince, may seem to oppose a dear friend that is an open enemy to his prince, because he dare do no other. [He does] not dare openly to entertain him, [but] openly appears against him; but yet his heart is towards him, and there is a secret, friendly correspondence. If there be an opportunity secretly to show him kindness, [he will] stand for 'im and plead, and extenuate, as far as he dares. Thus sinners [do].

But the saints do far otherwise: [they] oppose [sin] openly and secretly; [they have] no secret allowance, hiding [it] as a sweet morsel; [they have no] idol in a secret place, as Achan [did] the accursed thing [Josh. 7]. [A saint] will not, as far as he dares, stand up for it, and plead for it, palliate and excuse. Saints oppose sin as utterly rejecting and renouncing of it, as a man is ready to [reject] his enemy.

Sinners {fail to do so}, not in renouncing, but only in restraining.

Saints will not consent to give sin any quarters, to entertain it at all. {They} would have sin turned quite out.

But sinners [do not so].

Saints, {in opposing corruption in their hearts}, seek the perfect destruction of sin. [They are] not afraid of being too cruel. Sinners, {in opposing corruption}, take pity as it were; it grieves 'em to be so harsh with their lusts.

Saints oppose sin from the bottom of their hearts: [they] love to oppose it; don't desire that God should give 'em any leave; are glad that God don't allow it all; love the law of God on that account; love God because his nature is so infinitely contrary to sin; would oppose sin if there were no threatening; look on sin as their misery; treat it as a man would do a toad or serpent or some loathsome, venomous creature that {mankind} has a natural antipathy to.

But sinners [do not oppose sin].

Sixth. {In the opposition that is in the hearts of the} saints, {sin is not only opposed, it} is irreconcilable.

[They are] quite out with sin; [they] never will be reconciled any more [to it]. [They have] broke with it forever, finally renounced it without any intention or hopes of ever being friends with it anymore, with sincere desires of never having anything more to do with it. And therefore, the opposition continues everlastingly.

[But 'tis] not so with {sinners; with them, sin is not irreconcilable}. [They] may seem to oppose it very much for a season. There may [be] a great struggle in their minds under awakenings; [they] may exert themselves much against sin in many respects. But after a while, the seeming difference is made up again; all the while, there was a secret principle of friendship. Friendship never [was] utterly broke; [there remained] an entire regard to sin at bottom. And therefore, when times change, there is a reconciliation again. As when a father falls out with his child, or when lovers fall out, that have yet remaining a rooted, strong regard one to another.

Sinners are ready to be reconciled, [they are] only waiting for an opportunity. [They] are like the dog that has gorged his stomach with carrion: his stomach being overcharged, [it is] very loath [to lose] his food, and he may cast it up in a qualmish fit; but {he soon returns to it}.

Thus Judas seemed to forsake all. So Demas [II Tim. 4:10]. [Sinners are] like Pharaoh.

Seventh. Another difference, which follows from what has been now said, {in the hearts of the} saints, {is that} the longer the opposition against sin continues, the more it increases; but 'tis contrariwise {with sinners}.

[In saints, the] heart grows more and more tender, more and more sensible of the pain, more apt to be alarmed, dreading more the appearance of evil.

But {with} sinners, {the longer the opposition to sin continues, the} more and more hard and senseless {they become}.

{In the hearts of the} saints, {the more they oppose, the more} sin looks more and more dreadful; their enmity against it increases, and so their vigor and opposition {to sin}.

But ['tis the opposite with sinners].

{In the} saints, {the longer the opposition to sin continues, their hearts} grow stronger against [it]. [Their] hearts [become] more and more established {in grace; in them}, the house of David [grows] stronger and stronger.

But {with sinners, 'tis the opposite}.

This brings me to the

Eighth and last thing that I shall mention, wherein the difference {between saints and natural men lies in the manner of their opposition to sin}: and that is in the event and issue of the opposition. The issue {in the opposition} in the saints, is victory {over their corrupt principles}. But {in sinners, the issue} is sin's getting the victory.

Grace finally gets the victory over {corruption in saints}. The struggle may be very violent, {and} corruption may rage very much. All the powers of hell are on its side, and the innumerable tempting objects and occasions of this world are on its side. But yet, {grace} gets the victory.

[A] great character of true grace, [is] that it is victorious; the saints are they that overcome. God gives 'em the victory. I Cor. 15:57, "Thanks be to God, [which giveth us the victory through our Lord Jesus Christ]." II Cor. 2:14, "[Now thanks be unto God, which always causeth us to] triumph in Christ Jesus."

God has promised: [he] will subdue Satan under your feet; [he] will not quench the smoking flax, Matt. 12:20. Thus Jacob [is] finally promised;

[so] the children of Israel, [and the] house of David. Herein appears the power of godliness. The reason is, that God is in it, and God is on its side.

But as to {the opposition in} sinners, {the event and issue is that} sin at last gets the victory over conscience and self-love, and all that opposition that sinners make against it. Sin in them has their nature wholly on its side, and nature will get the victory. A stone may be forced upwards, a stream may be stopped, [but eventually nature will get the victory].

The enemies of sinners are stronger than they, {and overcome them}. Sin still has its life while in it, {and sin} is in reigning power; and therefore {it gets the victory}.

Sinners are miserable captives to sin and Satan. John 8:34, "a servant of sin." Rom. 7:14, "I am carnal, sold under sin." Like a bird that fowlers make use [of] to draw others, {which is} held on a string. {Or} like a mouse that is taken by her enemy, {which} is let go and runs for its life time after time, but is taken again, and is but the sport of its enemy, till at length {it} is devoured.

In that struggle that is between grace and corruption in the saints, the saints for the present don't get the victory as they would: {for} sin in some respects is too hard for them, {and reigns} so far as still to continue, {and 'tis} not abolished for the present. [Sin] still maintains some influence; still greatly molests, troubles and hinders the saints from doing as they would. Rom. 7[:15–16], "For that which I do I allow not: for what I would, that do I not; but what I hate, that do I. If then I do that which I would not, I consent unto the law that it is good."

But sin don't prevail in the manner that it does in sinners. In them, {sin} so prevails and has the upper hand, that it goes on still to reign {in them}, and finally prevails so as to fulfill its will.

[There are] two ways principally, wherein sin is wont to get the victory {in sinners}: either,

1. By their returning to the same sins again that they formerly went on in.

Thus it is oftentimes when men [are] opposed [by] a particular lust, when the temptation returns, when they have been opposing, and for a while refrain[8] from many sins. [Sometimes, they refrain] through convictions, {but they} return again. [They return] either by gradually losing

---

8. MS: "Refrains."

convictions and growing careless about their souls, or through a false hope. Or,

2. By sin's being turned into a new channel, as when a stream of water is opposed.

Thus it often is [with sinners]. Their case is no better than before. Sin has the victory; they are still miserable captives.

But in the opposition {that is in the hearts of the} saints, {and the issue of it}, they are conquerors; grace gets the victory. [They] refrain {from sin}, and [it] returns no more. 'Tis their manner to get the victory in times of temptation. Nor do they change one sin for another. And so sin is more and more mortified, till it is at length totally rooted out.

Here, before I conclude this *Use*, I desire this may be observed, lest true saints should be needlessly stumbled: and that is that there is in saints both those kinds of opposition to sin, viz., both of natural conscience and self-love, and also of grace. And therefore, none have any cause to be stumbled, that they found some things in them agreeable to the description given of the former, provided they find something further: {provided they} find those things that have been declared of the latter, wherein it goes beyond the former.

For instance, {true saints have} no cause of stumbling, partly from respect to the consequences of sin. Sometimes, their opposition to sin is partly forced. But yet those other things must be forced, {those things} that are peculiar to {natural conscience and self-love}.

[There is] opposition of heart, [opposition] of nature, that is free, [arising] from appetite [or] abhorrence. [Opposition must come] on its account: universally, utterly, finally, irreconcilably, [so that it is] increasing, victorious. For God's strength is made perfect in their weakness [II Cor. 2:19]. [Hence we see] God ordaining strength in babes and sucklings, because of his enemies [Ps. 8:2].

Use II of *Exhortation*.

First. To sinners, to strive earnestly that they may obtain the grace of God to oppose and resist that corruption that is in their hearts.

1. Consider that in the state that you are now in, you are wholly under the tyranny of corruption.

[There is in you] nothing that is good.

[The] reason is, that there is no love to God.

[There is] no good, but all manner of corruption.

2. Consider that while you continue without any grace to resist your corruptions, you are miserable captives and slaves to the devil. II Tim. 2:26, "taken captive by him at his will."

3. Consider what the corruption that is in your heart is like to bring you to, if you obtain no contrary principle to resist and overcome it.

It is a deadly disease.

Sin and Satan are cruel masters.

You are a friend to your lusts, but they are not friends to you. These masters deal otherwise by you, than you do by them. You seek to please them, yield to their desires, gratify 'em to your utmost, seek to advance and honor 'em, are careful of 'em, [and] can't bear to be cruel to 'em; [but they do otherwise by you].

Second, of exhortation to the saints, vigorously to maintain this warfare against the corruption of their hearts, that corruption may be weakened, and grace may grow.

Maintain a constant and earnest conflict with all your lusts,

Grace grows in this way. As a king that is at war with another increases his dominion, by fighting and by conquest, you [...]⁹

SERMON APPENDIX

1. Endeavor to fix your resolutions, [like] a soldier in war.
2. Observing your opportunities, and being seasonable in improving them.

Eccles. 9:10, "Whatsoever thine hand [find to do, do it with thy might]." Seek God early. Hos. 5. 15, "In their affliction they will [seek me early]." Is. 55:6, "Seek the Lord while he may be found."

3. Keep up a diligent watch.

I Pet. 5:8, "Be sober, be vigilant." Luke 21:36, "Watch and pray always."

4. In earning[10] and disposing things well.

Eccles. 9:18, "wisdom [is] better than weapons." Jer. 4:22, "[they are] wise to do evil, [but to do good they have no knowledge]."

Putting yourselves under advantages.

Avoid disadvantages.

Improving advantages.

---

9. MS breaks off.
10. Conjectural reading.

5. Wrestling with God.

6. Vigorous[ly] performing every part of your work.

That you may say as the Apostle, I Cor. 9:26, "I so run, as not uncertainly"; and as II Tim 4:7–8, "I have fought a good fight, I have finished my course, I have kept the faith: henceforth there is laid up for me a crown of righteousness, which the Lord, the righteous judge, shall give me at that day: and not to me only, but unto all them also that love his appearing."

You are not to expect it in any other way.

It never does grow any other way.

It grows in the hearts of all the saints.

But it is in this way.

The more vigorous this way is, the more will grace grow.

The great advantages of this growth.

(1) You come more and more into a state of blessed liberty.

CHRIST AND BELIEVERS ONE MYSTICAL PERSON
(Gal. 3:16, 1746)

IN EARLY 1746, EDWARDS PREACHED SEVERAL SERMONS THAT TREATED the nature of the Trinity. In March, the first person was considered in the sermon on I Corinthians 11:3 (no. 813),[1] and the second and third persons, respectively, in sermons on I John 4:14 (no. 818)[2] and Gal. 3:13–14 (no. 819),[3] from April. The present sermon seems to be a lead-in of sorts, or at least to bear some relation to Edwards' trinitarian considerations at this time.

He here examines the ways in which believers are looked upon by the Father as united to Christ in "one mystical person." The Explication of the text, Galatians 3:16, on the "seed of Abraham," harks back to a sermon of a few months earlier (no. 797, on Hebrews 2:16), and extends the argument of the oneness of Christ and believers because they are all of the spiritual posterity of Abraham. This sacred constitutional identity is laid down in certain divine covenantal "transactions," primarily the covenants of redemption and of grace. There is the covenant that God made with Christ as the second Adam or federal head; and there is a "marriage" covenant or contract that substantiates the joining of the "elect church" and Christ by virtue of Christ's purchase and exaltation. The "primary grounds" of this

---

1. Published as *God the Father* in *WJE* 25:142–54.

2. "The concern that the second person in the Trinity has in the affair of our redemption is this, that he is appointed of the Father to be the Savior of mankind." Apr. 1746. Refers to sermons on I Cor. 11:3 (no. 813) and Gal. 3:13–14 (no. 819).

3. See pp. 122–32.

mystical union is the act of the Father and Son, the "secondary grounds" the act, or "fruit," of believers. With its emphasis on union and covenant, therefore, this sermon relates to Edwards' view on justification.

The importance of these themes is indicated by content parallels in Edwards' private notebooks. He refers to this sermon (along with the one on Psalm 111:5 [Aug. 1745, no. 788]) at the end of "Miscellanies" no. 617, on the covenant of grace.[4] "Notes on Scripture" no. 421, which is cited in "Miscellanies" no. 824, treats Galatians 3:16, the text of this sermon.[5] The "Blank Bible" entry on this scripture provides the content of the Exposition for this sermon.[6] Finally, Edwards' private reflections in the "Discourse on the Trinity" (*WJE* 21:109–44) and "On the Equality of the Persons of the Trinity" (WJE 21:145–48) resonate strongly with his homiletic remarks on Galatians 3:13–14, and with other sermons on the teachings of the Trinity.

* * * * *

The manuscript, dated "Feb. 1745, 6" on the first page, is eighteen duodecimo leaves of mixed paper. The first leaf is made from a discarded letter to Edwards from Thomas Stevens of Plainfield, dated 25 Sept. 1745 (WJEO 32, Letter B55). An aborted, deleted beginning of another sermon, with I Corinthians 12:12 as the text, is on the second leaf. L. 15 is made from a discarded prayer bid. At the end of the sermon, Edwards wrote "Confession," meaning that an unnamed member of the church who was subject to church discipline was to have an opportunity to confess their fault before the congregation.

---

4. *WJE* 18:151.
5. *WJE* 15:500.
6. *WJE* 24:138, 1081–82.

Christ and Believers One Mystical Person

GALATIANS 3:16

He saith not, And to seeds, as of many; but as of one, And to thy seed, which is Christ.

THE OBSERVATION OF THE APOSTLE IN THESE WORDS, AT FIRST VIEW, MAY seem impertinent. The place referred to is Gen. 22:17–18, "an[d] thy[1] seed shall possess the gate of his enemies: and in thy seed shall all the nations of the earth be blessed." [This is] predicated of his seed nowhere else. [The seed is] spoken of in such a manner, that it is most naturally understood, not as a noun of multitude, or as containing a plurality, but only an individual, because of the singular verb *possess*, and the singular pronoun *his*. {It is} not usual in Scripture for a singular pronoun {to be annexed to the word "seed" when it is a noun of multitude}. [There is] something peculiar in the case. That seed of Abraham, in whom all the families of the earth should be blessed, is spoken of elsewhere as a single person, Ps 72:17. The word "seed" in Scripture [is] sometimes meant of a particular person. So Eve, on occasion of the birth of Seth, Gen. 4:25, says, "God hath appointed me another seed instead of Abel, whom Cain slew." So Hannah says, I Sam. 1:11, "If thou wilt give thine handmaid a man-child"; in the original it is "seed of man." [See a] parallel instance, Gen. 3:15, "And I will put enmity between you and the woman, and between your offspring and hers; he will crush your head, and you will strike his heel."[2]

1. I.e., Abraham.

2. The Exposition is virtually identical to the "Blank Bible" entry on Gal. 3:16 (*WJE* 24:1081–82), which provides the wording for insertions. The leaf on which this portion

Christ and Believers One Mystical Person

[The] Apostle don't mean that the promises were made only to Christ personally, v. 14, in opposition to a notion the Judaizing Christians in Galatia had entertained, that some inherited the blessings by faith, {and} some by the works of the law. [There is] no distinction of Jew nor gentile; so, agreeable to vv. 28–29, "There is neither Jew nor gentile, neither slave nor free, nor is there male and female, for you are all one in Christ Jesus. If you belong to Christ, then you are Abraham's seed, and heirs according to the promise."

DOCTRINE

In the divine transactions and dispensations relating to men's salvation, Christ and believers are considered as it were as one mystical person.

I. Very briefly explain [the Doctrine].
II. In what divine transactions and dispensations [Christ and believers are considered as one].
III. The grounds of it.

I. Explain [the Doctrine] in a few words.
First. [It is] not a proper, personal union, but [believers are] so united to Christ, and belonging to him, that they are regarded as though Christ and they were one, and they parts of him.

[Believers are] members [of Christ].

[They are] called Christ in the text. So again, I Cor. 12:12.

They are included in his name. Rev. 14:10, "presence of the Lamb."

Christ is said to be brought forth [by the church]. Rev. 12:5, "She gave birth to a son, a male child, who will rule all the nations with an iron scepter. And her child was snatched up to God and to his throne."

Christ is persecuted [in her name]. Act. 9:4, "Why persecutest thou me?" II Cor. 1:5, "For just as we share abundantly in the sufferings of Christ, so also our comfort abounds through Christ." [II Cor.] 4:10, "We always carry around in our body the death of Jesus, so that the life of Jesus may also be revealed in our body." Col. 1:24, "Now I rejoice in what I am suffering for you, and" fill up the suffering of Christ.

What is done to them, [is] spoken of as done to him.

---

of the sermon is written is made from a discarded letter to JE from Thomas Stevens, 25 Sept. 1745 (*WJEO* 37, Letter B55).

*Second.*³ They are looked upon as thus united by God {through Christ}, and so they are considered or regarded in the divine transactions, in all, unless those of God that establish the union, that are the grounds of their being thus respected,⁴ of which I shall speak at need.⁵

II. In what divine transactions [Christ and believers are considered as one].

First. Christ and the saints, or those that are chosen to be saints, are respected as one mystical person in that covenant that God has entered into, in order to their salvation. This [is] spoken of in the text. This is the first transaction, wherein [the] foundation of all the rest [consists]. In this covenant transaction, {Christ and believers are} considered as one, [as] in the covenant God made with Adam. {And} so in the *other* covenant, of which Christ is the head, that took place when the other failed.

But here, in order to rightly and distinctly understanding this matter, it must be observed that it is not thus in every covenant transaction between God and believers, in order to their salvation, that they are considered or respected as one mystical person. And therefore, it must here be carefully observed, that there is a twofold covenant transaction that God enters into, in order to the salvation of the elect.

1. There is the covenant that God entered into with Christ as the second Adam. There is such a covenant made with Christ, a covenant made with Abraham's seed, spoken of in the text. Ps. 89:28, "my covenant shall stand fast with him"; vv. 34–35, "My covenant will I not break, nor

---

3. The numeral for this head appears at the beginning of the fourth line of this passage; JE apparently decided to fill in the wording of the head, and so had to write above the numeral.

4. MS: "Respects."

5. The bottom of L. 2v. contains an aborted beginning of another sermon, the text of which appears upside down, which JE deletes with diagonal lines:

Feb. 1745, 6

---

1 Cor. 12. 12 . — so also
is Christ.

There are two things
taught in these words
viz the union of believers
one with another
and the union of them all
with Christ

Christ and Believers One Mystical Person

alter the thing that is gone out of my lips. Once have I sworn by my holiness that I will not lie unto David." Zech. 6:13, "[the] covenant[6] of peace shall be between them." Christ is our covenant head, as Adam was. God entered into covenant with him, in like manner.

This is the same with the covenant of redemption. This, and this only, is that which takes place instead of the first covenant with Adam.

This is the second covenant, as it takes effect in the second place, though first in the order of time. ['Tis] meet it should be so. This is the eternal covenant; ['tis] meet it should be from eternity.

This don't properly take [the] place of the covenant of works: for this is a covenant of works. Both the covenants, the first and the second, that made with the first Adam and that made with the second Adam, is a covenant of works.

2. There is another covenant between Christ and believers, as two contracting parties, in order to their union. ['Tis] represented in Scripture as a marriage covenant. This is distinct from the other. [There are] different parties contracting: God the Father is a party, only as concurring with his Son, and confirming [it]. [The two covenants have] different terms: that, works; this, faith.

And here I would observe, that this is that which is properly called the covenant of grace. [The] covenant [of] grace [is] everywhere in Scripture represented by a marriage covenant; but this is entirely different from God's covenant with the second Adam. This don't properly succeed in the room of the covenant with Adam: it is a covenant uniting men with their covenant head. Under the first covenant, [they were by] nature united. But here, grace succeeds to nature.

Now, it must be here observed, that it is not in this latter covenant that Christ and the elect are considered as one mystical person. Two distinct parties [are] contracting, in order to their union, but not considered as already united. I observed before {that Christ and believers are considered} as one mystical person in all transactions, excepting those {under the first Adam}. But in that other covenant, viz., the covenant God enters into with Christ as the second Adam, Christ and the elect are considered as one mystical person, that is spoken of in the text. Here, both are one side; one party are in the covenant, and God the Father the other, as Adam and his posterity were one party. In what Christ did in this covenant, he

---

6. KJV reads "counsel."

presented himself before the Father as a public person, as one including all the elect. [He] stood before the Father and entered into covenant as representing them, covenanting for himself and for them together in one.

In his engagements.

[Christ] engaged for them.

And in what the Father did: [he] looked on the elect as all as it were included in Christ in that transaction.

[The] promises were made to 'em as one: all to Christ mystical. Tit. 1:2, "God, that cannot lie, promised before the world began." II Tim. 1:9, "given us in Christ before the world began." [The Father] promised he should be released, acquitted, {that he would} justify [and] raise [him] from the dead, [and] give eternal life. [He] promised eternal life no other way.

[Christ would] ascend into it.

There enjoy him.

[He] should there reign, conquer his enemies: [the] devil, [and] enemies on earth; subdue [them] under his feet; judge the world. All the rewards God promised to Christ, were promised to Christ mystical.

God promised his Son in the eternal covenant {made with him}, that if he {fulfilled it}, his elect should have {eternal life}. And this was the way that he promised him, promised those benefits to him, and to them in him: the same way that God promised the eternal life of Adam's posterity to him, on condition {of fulfilling the covenant of works}. [They were] chosen in Christ before the world began. Eph. 1:4, "According as he hath chosen us in him before the foundation of the world, that we should be holy and without blame before him in love."

Second. Christ and his elect church are respected as one mystical person, in the purchase that Christ made. [He] acted for himself, and for them, in one. All that Christ purchased was for Christ mystical: deliverance for himself and them; release from the law; release from guilt. [He] merited in the first place for himself, and then for his elect as being as it[7] were parts of himself. Thus he merited and purchased {for the elect}.

Third. {Christ and believers} are considered as one in that which God bestowed on Christ, and which Christ took possession of after his humiliation. Rom. 8:34, "[It is Christ that died,] yea rather, that is risen again, [who is even at the right hand of God, who also maketh intercession

---

7. MS: "at."

for us]." Eph. 1:3-4, "Blessed be the God and Father of our Lord Jesus Christ, who hath blessed us with all spiritual blessings in heavenly places in Christ: according as he hath chosen us in him before the foundation of the world, that we should be holy and without blame before him in love."

Fourth. {Christ and believers are considered as one}, in the things which God doth to believers, or make them the immediate subjects of. Hitherto, I have spoken of those things which Christ is the more immediate subject [of]: [the] covenant, purchase, exaltation. In these, Christ and the elect are considered as one mystical person, as Christ is the subject of those things not by himself, and as separated from the elect, but as one with them and in their name, and the subjects of in him.

I now also observe that in those things that believers are the immediate subjects of {in the covenant}, they are not considered as by themselves, but as in Christ, as belonging to him, and as dealt with in his name. And Christ is said to be the subject of the same things in them: [their] afflictions, their prosperity.

Christ looks on their afflictions as his own, and their prosperity as his; their injuries as his injuries. So when God accepts their prayers, their praises, 'tis in Christ's name. God accepts and rewards their good works.

III. {I shall show} the grounds of this.

[*First.* The] primary grounds {on which Christ and believers are considered as one mystical person}, do consist in the[8] act of the Father and Son.

[*Second.* The] secondary [grounds consist] in the act of believers.

[*First.* The] primary, in the act {of the Father and Son}. [I] observed before that Christ and the elect are respected as one in all those divine transactions that concern their salvation, unless those that are the grounds {of the first covenant with Adam}. Those are that follow:

1. God the Father's eternal donation of them to Christ. John 10:29, "My Father, which gave them me." Ch. 17:6, "I have manifested thy name unto the men which thou gavest me out of the world: thine they were, and thou gavest them me." V. 9, "I pray not for the world, but for them which thou hast given me; for they are thine." [V.] 11, "Holy Father, keep through thine own name those whom thou hast given me, that they may be one, as we are."

---

8. MS: "in things acts of this Covenant have d The."

2. Christ's love to them.

3. Christ's undertaking for them, and procuring as their head and representative.

4. Christ's putting [himself] in their place, in their nature.

5. Christ's entering into covenant with believers.

[*Second*.] That which is secondly [the grounds of Christ and believers being considered as one mystical person], is the fruit of believers' consenting to that covenant that was but now spoken of. Hereby the soul is united [to Christ]. 'Tis its actual unition. Hereby the soul is espoused to Christ, and so becomes her head and husband. Though given to Christ from eternity, and though {promised to him}, yet {they are} not actually in Christ till they have believed in him, not actually members of his body. They are aliens and strangers till {they have faith in Christ},[9] though such great things were done for them.

Those things forementioned, {whereby Christ and believers are considered as one mystical person}, are the primary grounds, because they are the first foundation of all. They are the cause why the elect have faith. Faith itself is from that source and spring. And those other things are the primary {grounds}, inasmuch as they are so much the foundation of all, that in many things God respects Christ and his elect as one mystical person on this ground, before their faith, as {in the covenant of grace}.

But yet, even in these things, faith is not to be wholly excluded from being the ground of the elect's and Christ's being considered in them as one mystical person, because provision is made in these things, that the elect shall in time become believers, shall be actually united; and if no such provision had been made, they and Christ in these transactions would not be looked upon as one. God the Father would not {look on Christ and believers as one, and} Christ would not {look on himself and believers as one}. It would not be consistent with the perfections of God, [his] wisdom, [his] holiness. And in some respects, {believers} are not treated as one in God's transactions, till after faith. God treats with Christ as one with them, and Christ with God before their faith, on the foundation of God's donation {before the world was}.[10] But God don't treat with

---

9. On faith as the ground of "unition" with Christ, see "Miscellanies" nos. 712–14, *WJE* 18:341–45; and on the two covenants and the ground of unity, see the sermon on Heb. 9:15, Jan. 4, 1740 (no. 534).

10. See "Notes on Scripture" no. 422, *WJE* 15:501.

Christ and Believers One Mystical Person

[believers] as one with Christ, nor does Christ treat them as one with himself, till after they have actually believed in him.

APPLICATION

I. {*Use* of *Examination*}, whether or no you are a believer.

First. Whether you have ever been broken off from the stock of the first Adam. In order to determine this, inquire whether you have ever thoroughly been broken off from a dependence on a mere human righteousness.

Second. Have you ever, with your whole soul, consented to the covenant of grace as a covenant of espousals between Christ and your soul? You have heard [Christ]; Christ has wooed you. Has your whole soul yielded? Is your heart truly united [to him]? Are you united after the manner of a rational, active being? [With your] whole soul? [For a] whole Christ? Has your heart been thoroughly weaned from all other lovers? In marriage, a woman {gives herself only to her husband}. Do you give to Christ a chaste heart? [A] virgin [heart]? Is your heart united not only to Christ's estate, but his person? Have you taken Christ, to share with him in all conditions, for better, for worse? [Have you] accepted of him, as to give up yourself to him? [Have you] consented to be his forever?

Third. [Inquire] whether the heart to Christ be such as agrees to that of a member of Christ. [Is the union] exceeding strict and close? [Is it a] natural union, so as to have your whole dependence? Is Christ become your life? Is it so, as to look on Christ as one? [Is] his honor your interest? Is it so as to be devoted to Christ, to have a heart to sacrifice your private interest to the honor [of Christ]? Thus the members of the natural body are devoted. Such an union to Christ, we are abundantly taught, is necessary. [He] that "hateth not father and mother, and wife, and children, and brethren, and sisters, yea, and his own life, he cannot be my disciple" [Luke 14:26].

Fourth. Examine whether there be a conformity [to Christ].

II. *Use* of *Exhortation*.

First, to all earnestly to seek the glorious and blessed union with Christ, whereby you may become as it were one mystical person with Jesus Christ. How wonder[ful] is it, that such as we should be admitted to so close a union with so great {a person}. You have heard some of the benefits of it. More particularly, consider:

1. How great that happiness and glory must be, that consists in partaking with Christ of his happiness and glory, as one of his members.

2. There will forever be mutual sweet love and conversation, and enjoyment answerable.

3. If Christ and you are one, then you and he, and God the Father, and all the saints on earth, and saints in heaven, will be one, John 17. You and the Father will be one. [You are the] saints, [gathered in] one head, Eph. 1:10.

There will be everything agreeable to it, to all eternity.

4. How sure and certain your happiness must needs be. [You are] certain to Christ. [Christ is] made over for you in the same promises, the same purchase. [He] received not only for himself. He is already justified; he is already possessed. You cannot fail. Your perseverance will be certain. He is in a confirmed state.

5. If you are not united, how dreadful the separation will hereafter appear to [you], when the midnight cry [is heard, and the] door shut.[11] Hereafter, when you "see Abraham and Isaac and Jacob, and all the prophets, in the kingdom of God, and you yourselves thrust out" [Luke 13:28], [how dreadful will that be].

The time will come, when you will see the evidences of the union. Then you will see, those things are real things. It will be dreadful [thing] then to be separated, kept off at a great distance, as not fit to come nigh; shut out as abominable and odious and accursed; thrust away, driven away, as the eternal object of hatred and wrath.

---

11. L. 15 is made from a discarded prayer bid, which reads:
Sarjeant Burt and his wife and
Children desires the Continuance of the
prayers of the Congregation for him
he being brought very Low: nere the grave
also Elezebeth King being sick with the
Long fever Dezires the prayers of the
Congregation for her. her Mother
dezires the Same.
No record of a member of the Burt family with the rank of Sargeant has been found; however, Jonathan Burt (b. 1671) died in Oct. 1745; Elkanah Burt (1717–86) served in King George's War; and his brother David Burt (c. 1723–93) was in service after the Louisburg campaign. Elizabeth King could have been Elizabeth Denslow King of Windsor, Connecticut, who married William King of Northampton in 1686; he died in 1728, and she in 1746.

And then, consider the consequences. [You will be] wholly cast away by God; [he will] take no care of the welfare [of your soul].

This mystical person, even Christ mystical, is all that will be saved out of this visible world. Christ mystical is the new creation. Only this tree, with its fruitful branches, shall[12] escape the flames.

6. Consider how Christ condescends to seek this union with you, as great a thing as it is.

Second. The exhortation may be to believers.

1. Adore the infinite riches of divine grace towards you, in buying you. How dear it cost Jesus Christ, and how unworthy was you of it.

2. Seek an increase of a cordial and vital union with Jesus. The legal and relative union can't be increased.

3. Do all that you can do in religion, in the name of Jesus Christ.

4. Walk worthy of Christ.

5. Behave suitably to the near relation you stand in to the other members of Christ. [You are] one body, one mystical person with them. "Members one of another," Rom. 12:5.

Thus you will be in the way to that land of love and peace, where whole mystical Christ shall dwell to all eternity; where, after all means of grace, and common gifts and faith and hope, do cease, charity or divine love, that every part of Christ mystical shall be united with every other, shall never fail, but remain and flourish in the highest perfection and in a degree unspeakable to all eternity.[13]

---

12. MS: "that shall."

13. At the end of the sermon, JE wrote, "Confession," as a reminder, most likely, that a member of the congregation under discipline was to confess their offense.

THE HOLY SPIRIT THE SUM OF THE BLESSINGS PURCHASED FOR US BY CHRIST

(Gal. 3:13, 1746)

DURING MARCH AND APRIL OF 1746, EDWARDS PREACHED A SERIES ON the Trinity. The previous two were sermons on I Corinthians 11:3 and I John 4:14 (nos. 813 and 818).[1] This installment, on the third person, is the last one. Each sermon has Edwards' references to the others in the trilogy, uniting them as a literary and doctrinal whole, with a practical view emphasizing each divine person's role in the work of redemption. Choosing Galatians 3:13–14 for his explication of the Holy Spirit in this "affair," Edwards contrasts the works of law and grace, stating that by the latter believers are delivered through Christ's redemptive work from the curse of the law, and receive the Holy Spirit by faith. The Spirit, therefore, in its "operations and fruits," is the "sum" of the blessing that Christ purchased for the elect.

The doctrinal portion of the sermon consists of "evidences" of the Doctrine and of "particulars." A long string of evidences in the text show the Holy Spirit as the "great subject of the promises in the covenant God has entered into," as Christ's legacy to the church, as the topic consistently spoken of by prophets, as the "communicative fullness" of Christ, as the "great blessing Christ received for believers at his ascension," as the reward Christ received as his exaltation, as the "great blessing actually bestowed" on Christ after completing the work of redemption, as the sum

---

1. See below, p. 122.

The Holy Spirit the Sum of the Blessings Purchased for Us by Christ

of all "good things" for which the saints pray, as that which dwells in believers, as an earnest of their inheritance in heaven, as that through which believers partake in Christ's body and blood, and as the ultimate of all the "great blessings insisted on in the offers and invitations of the gospel." From this well-developed litany that hints at Edwards' robust view of the third person, he then shows "particulars": things that are used as "means" of the application of redemption, as "preparatory" to it, and wherein the application of redemption actually consists, from regeneration to union with Christ to justification. Also, "the blessings of Christ's purchase are from the Spirit's operation" distinct from the other two persons. Indeed, the benefits of Christ's purchase are "all," "ultimately and immediately," from the third person, as are all spiritual life and blessedness. Spiritual life and blessedness consist in the indwelling of the Holy Spirit in the hearts of believers, "as the very inward principle of life and happiness," the fountain, water, sap, oil, and breath of the soul.

Edwards continues with an Application for this sermon in Uses of Information, Examination, and Exhortation. He concludes with a brief "Improvement of the Whole," that is, of the sermon triad, summarizing the distinct contributions of each person to the work of redemption as well as their common work, for which each person of the Trinity is to be glorified. The theme of this sermon resonates in other writings of Edwards, such as the *Treatise on Religious Affections* that was published the same year.[2]

* * * * *

The manuscript is twelve duodecimo-sized leaves. Edwards' date is "April 1746." The Redemption symbol appears on the first page. At the end of the sermon are his notations, "Lecture. Take into church," reminders to make an announcement.

---

[2]. *WJE* 2:236, "For so are things constituted in the affair of our redemption, that the Father provides the Savior, or purchaser, and the purchase is made of him; and the Son is the purchaser and the price; and the Holy Spirit is the great blessing or inheritance purchased, as is intimated, Galatians 3:13–14, and hence the Spirit is often spoken of as the sum of the blessings promised in the gospel."

The Holy Spirit the Sum of the Blessings Purchased for Us by Christ

GALATIANS 3:13-14

Christ hath redeemed us from the curse of the law, being made a curse for us: for it is written, Cursed is every one that hangeth on a tree: that the blessing of Abraham might come on the gentiles through Jesus Christ; that we might receive the promise of the Spirit through faith.[1]

THE GREAT OCCASION OF THE APOSTLE'S WRITING THIS EPISTLE EVIdently, is this: {that the Galatians were returning to the works of the law}. What the Apostle insists upon in this chapter with the Galatians is this, that Christians receive the blessings of Christ's purchase only by faith, and not by works of the law.

And the great argument he insists upon here to prove this, is that Christians receive the Spirit only through faith, and not the works of the law. Thus in the beginning of the chapter: "[O foolish Galatians, who hath bewitched you, that ye should not obey the truth, before whose eyes Jesus Christ hath been evidently set forth, crucified among you? This only would I learn of you, Received ye the Spirit by the works of the law, or by the hearing of faith?" vv. 1–2].

So again in the text, wherein I would observe three things:

1. The curse we are delivered from by Christ's redemption: {viz.,} "the curse of the law."

---

1. After the text, JE inserts: "See sermon on I Cor. 11:3 and I John 4:14," respectively, nos. 813 and 818, preached in March and April 1746, the former published as *Of God the Father*, WJE 25:142–54.

The Holy Spirit the Sum of the Blessings Purchased for Us by Christ

2. The blessing that Christ purchased for us, or which we are brought to by Christ's redemption: {viz., "the} blessing of Abraham," i.e., the blessing of the covenant of grace. The Apostle speaks expressly of the covenant God made with Abraham as the covenant of grace, in the words immediately following the text: "Brethren, I speak after the manner of men; Though it be but a man's covenant, yet if it be confirmed, no man disannulleth, or addeth thereto. Now to Abraham and his seed were the promises made. He saith not, And to seeds, as of many; but as of one, And to thy seed, which is Christ. And this I say, that the covenant, that was confirmed before of God in Christ, the law, which was four hundred and thirty years after, cannot disannul, that it should make the promise of none effect" [vv. 15–17].

3. Wherein this blessing of the covenant of grace that we are brought to by Christ's redemption consists, viz., in our receiving the Holy Spirit: "that we might receive the promise of the Spirit through faith."

DOCTRINE

The Holy Spirit, or the third person of the Trinity, in his operations and fruits, is the sum of the blessings that Christ purchases for us in the work of our redemption.

I have lately spoken particularly concerning the character that each of the two first persons in the Trinity sustain in the affair of our redemption.[2] I now {shall consider the character of the Holy Spirit}.

I. Mention several evidences of the Doctrine.

II. Show how it is so by an induction of particulars.

III. How the benefits of Christ are from the Spirit's operation and influence, otherwise than from the Father and the Son.

I. Evidences [of the Doctrine].

This is plainly taught in the text {we are upon}. But further,

First. [The Holy Spirit is] the great subject of the promises in the covenant God has entered into, relating to man's redemption. The Spirit of God is spoken of as the great thing promised by God the Father to the Son in the covenant of redemption. Luke 24:49, "And, behold, I send the promise of my Father upon you: but tarry ye in the city of Jerusalem, until

---

2. See preceding note.

ye be endued with power from on high." Acts 1:4, "And, being assembled together with them, commanded them that they should not depart from Jerusalem, but wait for the promise of the Father, which, saith he, ye have heard of me." Acts 2:33, "Therefore being by the right hand of God exalted, and having received of the Father the promise of the Holy Ghost, he hath shed forth this, which ye now see and hear." Is. 59:20–21, "And the Redeemer shall come to Zion, and unto them that turn from transgression in Jacob, saith the Lord. As for me, this is my covenant with them, saith the Lord; My spirit that is upon thee, and my words which I have put in thy mouth, shall not depart out of thy mouth, nor out of the mouth of thy seed, nor out of the mouth of thy seed's seed, saith the Lord, from henceforth and forever."

[A further evidence is] the great promise of the covenant of grace made by Christ to believers. [So] in the text. Acts 2:38–39, "Then Peter said unto them, Repent, and be baptized every one of you in the name of Jesus Christ for the remission of sins, and ye shall receive the gift of the Holy Ghost. For the promise is unto you, and to your children, and to all that are afar off, even as many as the Lord our God shall call."

[A further evidence is the] Spirit of promise. Eph. 1:13, "In whom ye also trusted, after that ye heard the word of truth, the gospel of your salvation: in whom also after that ye believed, ye were sealed with that holy Spirit of promise."

Second. The great legacy that Christ left to his church at his death.

Third. [It is] insisted on by the prophets as the grand blessing, wherein should consist that blessedness and glory that the church should be brought to in the latter days by the Messiah. Is. 32:15, "Until the spirit be poured upon us from on high, and the wilderness be a fruitful field, and the fruitful field be counted for a forest." [Ch.] 44:3, etc., "For I will pour water upon him that is thirsty, and floods upon the dry ground: I will pour my spirit upon thy seed, and my blessing upon thine offspring." Ezek. 36:27, "And I will put my spirit within you, and cause you to walk in my statutes, and ye shall keep my judgments, and do them." Ch. 39:29, "Neither will I hide my face [any more from them: for I have poured out my spirit upon the house of Israel, saith the Lord God]." Joel 2:28, "And it shall come to pass afterward, that I will pour out my spirit upon all flesh; and your sons and your daughters shall prophesy, your old men shall dream dreams, your young men shall see visions."

Fourth. This is represented as that wherein the communicative fullness of Christ consists. John 1:14, "full of grace"; [v.] 16, "of his fullness [have all we] received, and grace for grace."

That was by his being full of the Spirit. {The Father} giveth not the Spirit by measure unto him. God the Father gave the Son his fullness, by appointing him.

Saints are made holy and happy by his unctions flowing down. Ps. 133:[2], "[It is like the precious ointment upon the head, that ran down upon the beard, even Aaron's beard: that went down to the] skirts of his garments." This is that which Christ communicates as a vital head.

[*Fifth.*] This is represented as the great blessing Christ received for believers at his ascension into heaven. John 16:7, "[Nevertheless I tell you the truth; It is] expedient for you that I go away." Acts 2:33, "[Therefore being by the right hand of God] exalted, and having received of the Father the promise of the Holy Ghost."

Sixth. Christ's own exaltation and glory he received as his reward, {and is represented as} chiefly consisting in [it]. Ps. 45:7, "[God hath] anointed thee with the oil of gladness." "[Thou shalt make them] drink of the rivers of thy pleasures" [Ps. 36:8].

Seventh. This was the great blessing actually bestowed, whereby Christ's promised success was fulfilled after he had finished the work of our redemption. Eph. 4:8, "When he ascended up on high, he led captivity captive, and gave gifts unto men."

Eighth. [This is] spoken of as the sum of all good things that we have to pray for. Luke 11:13, "how much more shall your heavenly Father give the Holy Spirit [to them that ask him]?" Matt. 7:11, "[how much more shall your Father which is in heaven give] good things [to them that ask him]?"

Ninth. 'Tis by the Spirit of God that God dwells in believers, and is bestowed on them as their portion.

Tenth. What the saints have of the Spirit of God in this world, is spoken of as the earnest of that inheritance Christ purchases for 'em. Eph. 1:13–14, "In whom ye also trusted, after that ye heard the word of truth, the gospel of your salvation: in whom also after that ye believed, ye were sealed with that holy Spirit of promise, which is the earnest of our inheritance until the redemption of the purchased possession, unto the praise of his glory." II Cor. 1:20–22, "For all the promises of God in him are yea, and in him Amen, unto the glory of God by us. Now he which stablisheth us with you in Christ, and hath anointed us, is God; who hath also sealed us, and given the earnest of the Spirit in our hearts." Ch. 5:4–5, "For we that are in this tabernacle do groan, being burdened: not for that we would be unclothed, but clothed upon, that mortality might be swallowed up of life. Now he that hath wrought us for the selfsame thing is God, who also hath given unto us the earnest of the Spirit."

Eleventh. We are spoken [of] as being made partakers of Christ's body and blood, by our receiving this. John 6:53, etc., "The Jews therefore strove among themselves, saying, How can this man give us his flesh to eat? Then Jesus said unto them, Verily, verily, I say unto you, Except ye eat the flesh of the Son of man, and drink his blood, ye have no life in you." V. 63, "It is the spirit that quickeneth; the flesh profiteth nothing: the words that I speak unto you, they are spirit, and they are life."

Twelfth. All the great blessings insisted on in the offers and invitations of the gospel. John 7:37–39, "[In the last day, that great day of the feast, Jesus stood and cried, saying, If any man thirst, let him come unto me, and drink. He that believeth on me, as the scripture hath said,] out of his belly flows rivers of living water." "[And he said unto me, It is done. I am Alpha and Omega, the beginning and the end. I will give unto him that is athirst of the fountain of the] water of life freely" [Rev. 21:6]. "[Ho, every one that thirsteth, come ye to the waters, and he that hath no money; come ye, buy, and eat; yea,] come, buy wine and milk [without money and without price," Is. 55:1].

II. Show how it is so by an induction of particulars.

First. Those that are used as means of the application of redemption, [such as] God's word.

Second. Those things that are preparatory to the application of redemption. John 16:8, "And when he is come, he will convince the world of sin."

Third. Those things wherein the application of redemption does consist:

Regeneration.

Union with Christ.

Union of hearts [in] love. Rom. 5:5, "And hope maketh not ashamed; because the love of God is shed abroad in our hearts by the Holy Ghost which is given unto us."

Faith. Gal. 5:22, "But the fruit of the Spirit is love, joy, peace, longsuffering, gentleness, goodness, faith."

The Holy Spirit the Sum of the Blessings Purchased for Us by Christ

Relative union.

Vital union.

As the union with Christ, so all the benefits that flow from it.

Justification.

Three ways:

[1.] Condition.

[2. The] sentence of justification pronounced in the Scriptures.

[3. A] sense of it in the conscience, removal of guilt from the conscience.

Not only justification, but adoption. [The believer is] qualified as a child [of God]. [He is] declared and manifested to be a child.

[Every believer] receives the spirit of a child. Gal. 4:5[-6], "To redeem them that were under the law, that we might receive the adoption of sons. And because ye are sons, God hath sent forth the Spirit of his Son."

[Every believer] is dealt with as a child:

Children's bread.

Manifestation of love.

Fatherly protection.

Fatherly guidance and instruction.

[The] work of grace [is] carried on:

[By] all spiritual light.

Life.

Strength.

Consent.

Help against temptations.

All holy intercourse with God and Christ in the duties of religion.

Blessing 'em always.

All things turn to their good through [the Spirit's] influence.

Through this, they have the good of temporal blessings:

Of affliction.

Perseverance.

Growth in Christ.

Final conquest.

Support and peace at death.

[Through this, they have the] glory and happiness of heaven. As is evident, because {of the} earnest of the Spirit.

[The] river of living water is the Spirit of God.

This is the great offer of the gospel: [the] perfect holiness of heaven, perfect joys.

[Through this, they have] the resurrection of the body. Rom. 8:11, "[But if the Spirit of him that raised up Jesus from the dead dwell in you, he that raised up Christ from the dead shall also quicken your mortal bodies by his Spirit that dwelleth in you]." [He is] the Spirit that quickens, John 6:63.

[Through this, they have the] glorification of the body. "[It is] raised a spiritual body," I Cor. 15:46.

"By his spirit [he] hath garnished the heavens; his hand hath formed the crooked serpent," Job 26:13.

Consummate glory and heaven.

As God's Spirit garnished the old creation, so and much more the new.

[Through this, they have] the eternal fellowship and communion of saints with Christ.

III. How the blessings of Christ's purchase are from the Spirit's operation, otherwise than from the other two persons of the Trinity.

Before [I] observed that it is of the Father that all {the blessings purchased for us by Christ} are obtained by redemption, that it is He that grants the things purchased {by Christ}. And that the Son is the Savior, not only as he obtained {the benefits}, but bestows and communicates [them].

Now the question is, [How are the benefits of Christ's purchase from the Spirit?].

Answer 1. The benefits of Christ's purchase are all by the Holy Ghost, the third person in the Trinity, ultimately and immediately.

[They] are from the Father primarily as he {grants the things purchased; they} are from the Son, secondarily and immediately, as he {obtains, bestows and communicates them; and they are} from and in the Holy Ghost ultimately and immediately. [They are] of the Father, through the son. I Cor. 8:6, "one God, the Father, of whom are all things, and we in him; and one Lord Jesus Christ, by whom [are all things, and we by him]." And they are] all immediately in and by the Holy Ghost.

This variety of the way in which we have {the benefits of redemption} from the several persons of the Trinity, is probably what the Apostle has respect to when he says, Rom. 11:36, "For of whom, through whom, and to whom, are all things."

The Holy Spirit the Sum of the Blessings Purchased for Us by Christ

All is of the Father originally, as the head of all {the work of redemption}. All is through the Son, as the grand medium. All [is] by the Holy Spirit, in the immediate efficient. He appropriates [and] immediately possesses particular persons.

This diverse dependence on the several persons of the Trinity is spoken of by the Apostle. I Cor. 1:30, "of him are ye in Christ Jesus, who of God is made unto us wisdom, and righteousness, and sanctification, and redemption."

[*Answ.*] 2. All {spiritual life and blessedness} is from the Holy Spirit, as the messenger of the other two persons and their agent in the heart to execute their gracious designs, as subject to the other persons. [The Holy Spirit is subject] more immediately as the messenger of the Son, but is subjected to the Son by the Father in the head of all.

[*Answ.*] 3. The Scriptures don't only represent spiritual life and blessedness as immediately from the Spirit of God, but as consisting in his indwelling in the hearts and his action there. When I say "consisting in {his indwelling in the hearts}," I mean as the very inward principle of life and happiness.

'Tis the inward fountain of holiness in the heart, [a] well of living water. All spiritual life and holiness [are] summed up in divine love.

But the Spirit of God in the heart is spoken of as it were [as] the very fountain of love there itself. Gal. 5:13, etc., "For, brethren, ye have been called unto liberty; only use not liberty for an occasion to the flesh, but by love serve one another." 1 John 3, two last verses: "[And this is his commandment, That we should believe on the name of his Son Jesus Christ, and love one another, as he gave us commandment. And he that keepeth his commandments dwelleth in him, and he in him. And hereby we know that he abideth in us, by the Spirit which he hath given us]." Ch. 4:12–13, "No man hath seen God at any time. If we love one another, God dwelleth in us, and his love is perfected in us. Hereby know we that we dwell in him, and he in us, because he hath given us of his Spirit."

This is not only the immediate bestower of this water of life, but it is the very water of life itself.

The sap of the branch that it derives from the tree, is the very life of it.

But this is the very sap.

'Tis the very oil.

Christ is represented as [the] olive tree. {The Holy Spirit is represented as} the oil in the very sap and juice of the olive {tree}. Zech. 4:2, 6, "And said unto me, What seest thou? And I said, I have looked, and behold a candlestick all of gold, with a bowl upon the top of it, and his seven lamps thereon, and seven pipes to the seven lamps, which are upon the top thereof. [. . .] Then he answered and spake unto me, saying, This is the word of the Lord unto Zerubbabel, saying, Not by might, nor by power, but by my spirit, saith the Lord of hosts." With v. 12, "[And I answered again, and said unto him, What be these two olive branches which through the two golden pipes empty the golden oil out of themselves?"

[The] Spirit of God is in the soul, as the breath is in the body. Thus {the Holy Spirit is} called the breath of life. [The Spirit is] as the vital heat is in the body. The Spirit of God is the fullness of the creation, its life and glory. The fullness of rational creatures is not in themselves, but in God. Indeed, all that the Spirit of God does in order to the happiness of believers, is not in this manner. [He has] his common influences.

APPLICATION

Use [I.] of *Information*.

First. Hence one reason why our Savior has the name of the Messiah, or the Christ, given him in Scripture.

Second. Hence how great a blessing is the outpouring of the Spirit of God.

[*Use*] II [of] *Examination*, whether or no the Spirit of God has ever applied to you the redemption of Christ.

First. Have you ever been brought to see your dependence on the Spirit of Christ, that you are deformed and loathsome, blind, without strength, without true comfort, dead?

Second. Is the Spirit of God within you as a principle or inward spring of new life? Do you live in the Spirit?

Third. Does the Spirit of God communicate himself to you in his own proper nature? [The Holy Spirit is] pure spirit; [it is] compared to water that washes the body clean. [Believers are] baptized with water and the Spirit, [like] bodies washed with pure water.

Fourth. Do you delight in the things of the Spirit? Rom. 8:5, "they that are after the flesh do mind the things of the flesh." Are you not sensual, carnal?

Fifth. Is that principle within you, that you account the Spirit of God, powerful and fervent? [It is] compared to fire. Luke 24:32, "Did not our heart burn within us?"

Sixth. Above all things, examine whether you have the fruits of the Spirit. Gal. 5:[22]-23, "But the fruit of the Spirit is love, joy, peace, long-suffering, gentleness, goodness, faith, meekness, temperance."

[Do you have the] temper of Christ?

Use III of *Exhortation.*

First. To seek the Holy Spirit.

1. How miserable those are, that are without the Spirit.

2. How happy those are, that are spiritual fellows with the Father and Son. [They] make their abode [in them]; have heaven in them. [They] are the temples of God.

This is what you have to seek and strive for, above all things. In striving for this, you strive for the kingdom of heaven. You must part with all for this. This is the great blessing you have to pray for.

Second. Take heed you don't sin against the Holy Spirit. Such sins are, above all others, dangerous. [They] bring the greatest guilt. [They] harden the heart.

[Hardening the heart] opposes the Spirit of God in others, [and] resists the Spirit of God in yourself.

[Hardening the heart is] grieving and quenching the Spirit of God. [The] Spirit of God is grieved and quenched by sloth and negligence under his striving; by sinning against his convictions in the conscience, by backsliding after strivings, especially by pride and malice.

How dreadful have been the consequences of persons grieving and vexing the Holy Spirit. {So the} children of Israel in the wilderness; {so the} Jews in the apostles' days. Acts 7:11, "[ye do] always resist the Holy Ghost."

[This is] the way to be finally left of the Spirit of God How miserable has been the case of such as have been thus lost souls, {such as} Judas. How did David deprecate this, Ps. 51. The putting out the fire of the Spirit of God, is the kindling up the fire of God's wrath.

[IMPROVEMENT OF THE WHOLE]

[I shall] conclude with a few remarks from the whole that has been said concerning the distinct offices of each of the persons in the Trinity, and the different character that each one sustains, and the part he acts, in the great affair of our redemption.

First. How great a work the work of redemption is. How great is their sin, who neglect so great a salvation. How happy they who have an interest in it.

Second. How much is each person of the Trinity glorified in this work. Hence, how we ought to glorify each person.

Third. How great and universal our dependence is on God for salvation and happiness. I Cor. 1, three last verses, "[That no flesh should glory in his presence. But of him are ye in Christ Jesus, who of God is made unto us wisdom, and righteousness, and sanctification, and redemption: that, according as it is written, He that glorieth, let him glory in the Lord." [We depend on] each one, all in all. [So] the Father, I Cor. 15:28; [so] Christ, Col. 3:11.

Fourth. Hence the reason why we are baptized in the name of the Father, the Son and the Holy Spirit. How is that said to be this fruit of the vine, but that that is represented by this.

Fifth. Hence we may learn how to understand that apostolical benediction in II Cor. [13:14, "The grace of the Lord Jesus Christ, and the love of God, and the communion of the Holy Ghost, be with you all."]

Hence we see how very comprehensive this benediction [is], how even all good, all manner of well-being, every good they received or are capable of and can enjoy in time and eternity, is comprehended in this benediction.[3]

---

3. JE notes at end of sermon: "Lecture. Take into church."

SAVING FAITH WORKETH BY LOVE
(Gal. 5:6, 1751)

EDWARDS FIRST PREACHED THIS SERMON IN MARCH 1751 AT THE HOME of Noah Clark in Pascommuck, Massachusetts, and he re-preached it January 1752, while serving in Stockbridge after his expulsion from Northampton. The manuscript is typical of Edwards' later sermons, in that it consists of a fairly bare outline. Even so, he defends three propositions: that love is a distinguishing property of saving faith, that saving faith is love for God and man; and it is confirmed by works. He then concludes with a lengthy Application section that contains three sections of Information, Trial, and Exhortation.

One reason that this sermon is brief and very sparsely written is that it was written for a meeting in a private home. But Edwards could have elaborated on each telegraphic line to an unknown extent, which makes this a reference for a largely extemporized performance. Also, a comparison with a prior sermon on the same text in 1728 (no. 59) proves fruitful. For example, in both sermons Edwards presents a fairly similar Doctrine, identifying saving faith as consisting in love. However, in the first sermon, Edwards spent the majority of his time explaining the meaning of faith; in the latter, he primarily considers the nature of love that stems from saving faith. Consequently, in the earlier sermon Edwards defines the "three orders of true faith," while here he does not define faith but instead expounds the love that proceeds from faith.

Furthermore, the Application sections differ notably. In the first sermon, Edwards urges his hearers to focus on faith. Particularly noteworthy is Edwards' exhortation to *unbelievers* to seek faith by considering the excellency, pleasantness, usefulness, reasonableness, and necessity of faith. However, in the second, he urges *believers* to seek love and to examine themselves to ensure that such love to God and man is present.

The differences are possibly explained by Edwards' historical circumstances. Beginning in 1722, he reflected deeply on the meaning of justifying faith as indicated by the frequency of reflection found in the "Miscellanies." These reflections reached their climax in 1734 when he preached *Justification by Faith*, which inspired revival. It is unsurprising that, at that historical moment, Edwards more adamantly urged unbelievers to place their faith in Christ.

By 1751, the context was quite different. Edwards had been run out of his church, and had experienced great enmity from the flock of his charge in Northampton rather than the love that he believed should be characteristic of the Christian. Though he had a new position at Stockbridge, he returned to Northampton occasionally, since he had both family and friends there. But he was confined to preaching in the homes of a narrow circle of supporters. Furthermore, during this time period, Edwards had been reflecting on the nature and character of love as particularly located in the godhead (see, for example, "Miscellanies" no. 1180). Perhaps the reflection on divine love stimulated his conviction of the necessity of corresponding love in the lives of those who have saving faith in that triune God of love. It is not surprising, then, that Edwards would choose in this sermon to urge believers to pursue love with greater fervor than he did in his former sermon.

* * * * *

The manuscript is four duodecimo leaves. Edwards' inscription at the top the first page reads, "At Pascommuck, Noah Clarks March 1751." Written perpendicularly in the left margin is the repreaching date, "Jan. 1752."

Saving Faith Worketh by Love

GALATIANS 5:6

But faith which worketh by love.

1. The grace described.
2. [The] distinguishing nature and property of it.
3. The importance of it.

DOCTRINE

Tis a great and distinguishing property of a saving faith that it worketh by love.

Proposition I. All true faith is working faith.
['Tis] inwardly operative, productive of good works.
['Tis] a life of labor, activity and universal obedience.
First. From the reason of things.
The nature of all true grace.
The nature of faith in particular.
The nature of the Savior received; an holy Savior.
[The] nature of his office.
The way proposed of obtaining the future salvation.
Second. From the testimony of Scripture. Jas. 2:14, "What doth it profit, my brethren, though a man say he hath faith, and have not works? can faith save him?" [Vv.] 20, 26, "But wilt thou know, O vain man, that faith without works is dead? [. . .] For as the body without the spirit is dead, so faith without works is dead also."

Prop. II. Love ever attends and is implied in a saving faith.

First. Observe what love [is].
Second. The evidence of the proposition.

First. What love [is].
Answer in general: divine love, holy or Christian love.
[It] mortifies carnal affections.
1. Supreme love to God for their divine excellency and beauty.
A principle of divine love first appears in love to God.
This love is primarily for his own excellency.
This excellency especially as appearing in the face of Christ.
This love is supreme.
(1) Of benevolence.
(2) Of complacence.
2. A holy love to men.
Love of benevolence to all enemies.
Love of complacence to the saints.
Second. Evidence [of the proposition].
1. The nature of that knowledge that is the foundation of faith.
(1) Knowledge of the divine excellency and glory, Ps. 9:10.
(2) Knowledge of his goodness and grace; lovingkindness, Ps. 36:7.[1]
2. Nature of the principle and act of faith itself.
'Tis the whole soul's receiving Christ.
It has its special seat in the heart.
Prop. III. True faith is operative and effectual in good works by virtue of this divine love that is implied.
By this it is so powerful in its inner operations.
By this [it is] fruitful.
This is the life and soul.
This operative nature, without which it is dead.
If [I have] faith so that [I] could remove mountains, [yet am] without love, [I] are nothing [I Cor. 13:2].
Love is an active, operative principle.
Love and hatred are the springs of the soul's motions.
Natural love is powerful.
But divine love more powerful.

---

1. See sermon no. 989 on this text, preached the same month at a private meeting in Northampton.

APPLICATION

[*Use*] I [of] *Information*.

First. Hence true love makes a great alteration in persons, both in heart and life.

[It] not only gives comfort, [but] alters the temper, the behavior.

Second. What a happy life a life of true Christianity is.

That life which arises from these two principles of faith and love must needs be a happy life.

Faith gives a view of those things which [is] most glorious.

We here indeed live in a miserable world, but faith carries the soul as it were out of it into a better world; gives a view of the most excellent things of that world.

Love[2] gives a relish of them,

Unites the soul to them; implies a supreme complacence in them.

Faith enables the soul to rely on a future enjoyment of those things, to lay hold on the promises.

By faith the soul is enabled to see that there is so glorious a person as Jesus Christ. {The soul is enabled to see} such glorious things.

By love the soul cleaves {to Christ,} relishes.

By faith the soul has the comfort of a prospect of the full enjoyment.

One of these alone cannot make the soul happy.

Both together make the life of a Christian a truly happy life, I Pet. 1:8.[3]

[*Use*] II [of] *Trial*.

Try your faith.

Is [it] an active, powerful principle?

[Is it] productive?

[It] is accompanied with divine love?

Is love the life and soul of it?

Does it work by such a principle? [Does it] make this to be your nature? Are you a loving temper? Are principles of malice mortified?

Use III of *Exhortation*, to seek such a faith.

---

2. MS: "describe Love." This deletion is written upside down, indicating that JE had commenced writing on this side of the page but then abandoned it, reversed the page and started on the other side.

3. This part of the sermon is made of an undated fragment of a promissory note between JE and Prudence Stoddard for the sum of forty pounds; written on the other side of the paper in an unidentified hand is the memo, "Mr Edwards's B[ond?] / £20 ——."

Consider:
First. That nothing avails to any purpose without it.
Second. To what great and glorious purposes such a faith avails.
Avail to unite to Christ, of an interest in his righteousness.
For the pardon of all sin.
To bring into God's family.
To sanctify the soul.
To give that peace.
Unspeakable joy.
Rest and comfort in all the troubles and tumults of the world.
To enable you to walk suitably under all changes.
Spread a table in a wilderness.
Quietness in a strong tempest.
Peace at death.
Save from the power of the devil.
Happy after death.
To entitle you to a happy resurrection.
To perfect happiness and glory to all eternity.

www.ingramcontent.com/pod-product-compliance
Lightning Source LLC
Chambersburg PA
CBHW031502160426
43195CB00010BB/1071